AF317024

STEALTH WEALTH

The Ultimate Guide to Building and Protecting an Invisible Fortune

JEREMIAH J. BROWN

Stealth Wealth:

The Ultimate Guide to Building and Protecting an Invisible Fortune

Jeremiah Brown

ISBN: 979-8-21815-926-9

"Smart people see things for how they really are, while everyone else sees things for how they want them to be."

-WISDOM

THE POWER OF INFORMATION
Institutional ownership can't lose

In today's world, information is power. The ability to gather, analyze, and act on information can make all the difference in the pursuit of wealth. The events surrounding the collapse of Silicon Valley Bank and other small banks highlight this point. The bank's insiders and CEOs knew of the bank's impending doom and took their money out days before the bank collapsed. This is a clear example of the power of information and how it can be used to build wealth and take advantage of opportunities. For those in pursuit of stealth wealth, the importance of information cannot be overstated. The ability to access timely, accurate, and relevant information can help one make informed decisions and take advantage of opportunities that others may miss. The Silicon Valley Bank case illustrates this point perfectly. The insiders who knew of the bank's troubles were able to act on that information and protect their wealth. Those who did not have access to this information were left out in the cold.

The lesson here is clear: those who have access to information have a significant advantage over those who do not. This advantage is particularly important in the pursuit of wealth. To build wealth, one must be able to identify and take advantage of opportunities, and this requires access to the right information. But where can one find this information? The answer is everywhere. Information is all around us, and it has never been easier to access it. The internet, social media, news outlets, and even personal networks are all sources of information. The key is to know what information is relevant and how to use it. For those in pursuit of stealth wealth, it's important to focus on information that is relevant to their goals. This means staying up-to-date on industry trends, economic indicators, and market fluctuations. It also means building a strong network of like-minded individuals who can share insights and information.

But it's not enough to simply have access to information. One must also be able to analyze and act on it. This requires a certain level of knowledge and expertise. It's important to develop a deep understanding of the industries and markets one is interested in. This can be done through education, experience, and networking. In the end, the pursuit of stealth wealth is all about information. The ability to access, analyze, and act on information can make all the difference in building wealth and taking advantage of opportunities. The recent events surrounding the collapse of Silicon Valley Bank serve as a reminder of this fact. Those who had access to information were able to protect their wealth, while those who did not suffered the consequences. So, if you want to build wealth and achieve your financial goals, focus on gathering and utilizing information to your advantage.

"Your net worth is determined by what remains after subtracting your BAD habits from your GOOD ones."

CHAPTER 1:

The Origins of Stealth Wealth

THE GREATEST ECONOMIC RUG PULL OF OUR TIME

They say that if you want to predict the future, you should study history. If you followed this era of free money for too long (2011-22), you'll quickly realize that this version of irrational exuberance happened so many times before. It never ceases to amaze me how our society seems to always forget the historical facts of Federal Reserve policy and market cycles. However, imagine there being a group of individuals who saw the 2023 economic rug pull coming and took advantage of it. They knew that a decade of low-interest rates, quantitative easing (QE) printing, and a massive monetary expansion during the COVID-19 pandemic would lead to inflation and a nation of easy money, over-leverage, and speculation. They saw an opportunity not only to join in on the trends but also to position their portfolios to make a profit and get out right in time. Would you believe it? I do. They called themselves the "Stealth Wealthy." I call one of them Carl Icahn.

In response to the COVID-19 pandemic and the resulting government shutdowns, central banks around the world, including the US Federal Reserve, embarked on an unprecedented wave of monetary expansion. This involved the creation of massive amounts of new currency, and as much as 40% of all currency in existence was created out of thin air during this period! Yes, this is not a typo, 40% percent of every dollar used in all of existence was created in 2020! The Fed also introduced a bond-buying program and pushed the reserve requirements for banks (banks must have a minimum of 10% of a depositor's money available at any given time) to almost zero percent. The goal of this monetary expansion was to provide a lifeline to the economy, which was suffering from the devastating effects of the pandemic. However, as the economy began to recover, concerns began to grow about the potential impact of this monetary expansion on inflation. In response, the Fed announced plans to raise interest rates and stop its bond-buying program to control inflation. This move, commonly referred to as a "rug pull," being the most aggressive set of rate hikes in history, had significant implications for the economy, leading to overexposure of illiquidity and the end of an era of easy profits and irrational speculation.

The idea behind a "rug pull" is that it removes the safety net that has been put in place to support the market. In the case of the Fed's decision to raise rates and stop bond-buying, this safety net was the easy availability of cheap credit and currency. With this safety net removed, investors and traders were forced to reevaluate their positions and adjust their strategies, causing a period of volatility and uncertainty. One of the key ways in which this rug pull created a nation of easy money and speculation was through the impact it had on interest rates. With rates rising, borrowing became more expensive, which, in turn, led to a decrease in the demand for credit. This made it more difficult for businesses to access the capital they needed to grow and invest, which, in turn, led to a slowdown in economic growth. At the same time, the rug pull also had a significant impact on the stock market. With easy credit no longer available, investors were forced to reassess the value of the stocks they held. This led to a period of volatility as investors bought and sold stocks based on their changing perceptions of their value.

While the goal of the Fed's actions was to control inflation, the long-term impact of this move on the economy remains to be seen. So why do the few, such as Carl Icahn, who are often referred to by many as one of the "stealth wealthy," manage to always stay one step ahead of the economy? Well, after reading the next few chapters, you'll soon realize that the answers are as clear as a memory etched in stone.

Let us begin…

ORIGIN OF THE TERM "STEALTH WEALTH"

Stealth wealth refers to a financial lifestyle where individuals choose to keep their wealth and investments concealed and not flaunt them publicly. The term is often used to describe wealthy individuals who live a modest lifestyle and keep their investments low-key and hard to detect. They often focus on alternative investments such as real estate, private equity, hedge funds, or offshore accounts instead of traditional, more visible investments like stocks or bonds. More importantly, they are laser-focused on the overall economy, loopholes, and Federal Reserve policy changes. The idea is to maintain privacy, control, and stability of their wealth, avoiding attention from the media, government, or potential criminals.

The concept of stealth wealth is believed to have originated in the early 20th century during the industrial revolution. Today, we live in a world where appearance often matters more than substance. We are bombarded with images of wealth, success, and glamour on a daily basis. Social media, reality TV shows, and celebrity lifestyles have contributed to the notion that the road to financial freedom lies in ostentatious displays of wealth. But the truth is, many of the wealthiest people in the world choose to fly under the radar, investing their money in ways that are not immediately apparent. This is the concept of stealth wealth.

FLYING UNDER THE RADAR

So what is stealth wealth, and what does it mean to truly fly under the radar while building wealth?

Stealth wealth is the practice of keeping one's wealth hidden from public view, avoiding any conspicuous displays of affluence. This can be achieved through a variety of means, from investing in real estate or businesses that generate passive income to keeping one's net worth under wraps. The idea is to maintain a low profile, live below your means, and build wealth in a sustainable and discreet way. One of the key benefits of stealth wealth is that it allows individuals to live their lives without the pressure of public scrutiny or envy. However, in our pursuit of financial stability and wealth, it is not uncommon to encounter social challenges along the way. The perception of being "wealthy" can attract all sorts of pressures, such as being expected to spend more or being asked for monetary support from friends and family. So in theory, the motivations behind stealth wealth are largely 'personal' rather than financial. It provides a way to step out of the comparison game, where our worth is often measured by our financial status, and puts the power of financial decisions back in our hands.

By not constantly advertising one's financial strength, others are less likely to view them as a source of financial support or expect them to spend more. Stealth wealth empowers individuals to make each financial assessment and decision at their discretion, without being pressured by others. It provides a sense of privacy and security and the freedom to make investment decisions based on one's own values and goals, rather than trying to conform to society's expectations. Another advantage of stealth wealth is that it provides a level of insulation from the volatility of the financial markets. By diversifying investments into a range of assets and avoiding reliance on stocks or bonds, stealth wealth practitioners can minimize their risk and ensure a more stable financial future. But perhaps the most compelling reason to pursue stealth wealth is that it opens up the opportunity to live life on one's own terms. With passive income streams and a solid financial foundation, individuals can choose to work less, travel more, or pursue their passions without the constraints of a 9-to-5 job.

EXAMPLES OF STEALTH WEALTH

There are countless examples of successful individuals who have adopted the principles of stealth wealth to achieve financial freedom. Here are some of the most notable masters of stealth wealth:

Reginald Lewis was a self-made billionaire and businessman who rose to prominence in the late 20th century. Born in Baltimore, Maryland, in 1942, Lewis grew up in a working-class family and faced numerous obstacles on his path to success. Despite these challenges, he earned a scholarship to attend Virginia State University and later became one of the first African American CEOs of a Fortune 500 company. Lewis was a true master of stealth wealth, using his success in business to build a hidden fortune while maintaining a low profile. He was a savvy investor who always looked for undervalued assets and invested in companies that he believed had the potential for significant growth. He was also known for his frugal lifestyle, avoiding the trappings of wealth such as expensive cars and designer clothing and instead focusing on building his wealth through smart investments. Reginald Lewis is just one of many examples of individuals from communities of color who have embraced the principles of stealth wealth and achieved financial freedom. By following in his footsteps and adopting similar strategies, anyone can build their own stealth wealth and secure their financial future.

Steven Schwarzman and David Tepper are both extremely wealthy individuals with significant annual incomes. According to Forbes, Schwarzman had a net worth of $22.6 billion as of February 2021, and Tepper had a net worth of $12.4 billion. Although Schwarzman and Tepper may not be household names, their companies have significant influence in the financial world and are likely aligned with products or services that are well-known. For example, Blackstone has invested in a wide range of companies and industries, including real estate, energy, and technology. Some of the companies in Blackstone's portfolio, such as Hilton Worldwide and The Weather Channel, are well-known to the general public. Similarly, Appaloosa Management has invested in a wide range of companies, including technology firms like Alibaba and social media companies like Facebook. Despite their significant wealth, both Schwarzman and Tepper have demonstrated a commitment to philanthropy and giving back to society. This is a common trait among those who practice stealth wealth, as they often prioritize using their resources to make a positive impact rather than simply accumulating more wealth.

Carl Icahn is an American investor, businessman, and philanthropist who is widely regarded as one of the most successful and influential investors of all time. However, the activist investor employs various investment strategies and tactics that are NOT widely known or understood by the general public. For example, he may use complex financial instruments such as derivatives, options, and futures contracts to hedge his positions and increase his returns. He may also invest in private companies, partnerships, or other vehicles that are not subject to the same disclosure requirements as publicly traded companies. In addition to his investments, Icahn has been involved in a variety of businesses throughout his career, including real estate, energy, and gaming. He has also been known to engage in activist investing, in which he takes a significant stake in a company and uses his influence to push for changes that he believes will increase shareholder value.

British designer Jony Ive has a net worth estimated to be around $500 million. He made his fortune as a designer at Apple, where he worked for over 20 years and was responsible for the design of many of the company's most iconic products, including the iPod, iPhone, and iPad. Ive was known for his minimalist and sleek design aesthetic, which helped differentiate Apple's products from those of its competitors. In 2015, Ive was promoted to the position of Chief Design Officer at Apple, a newly-created role that gave him more responsibility for the company's overall design strategy. However, he maintained a relatively low profile and rarely gave interviews or made public appearances. Ive left Apple in 2019 to start his own design firm, LoveFrom, where he continues to work on various projects. Despite his immense wealth and influence, Ive has managed to maintain a level of privacy and discretion that aligns with the principles of stealth wealth.

These examples highlight the diversity of individuals who have embraced stealth wealth and successfully built substantial fortunes while avoiding the trappings of excessive fame and public attention. By following their lead and adopting similar strategies, anyone can cultivate their own path to financial freedom while maintaining privacy and control over their wealth.

So why do these people choose anonymity over being public-facing?

Personally, I believe it's because their experiences throughout their careers have made them aware of their social environments, and they are smart enough to realize that there is absolutely no benefit to being a public figure when weighed against the key elements of time, money, and effort required to maintain that status. There is a difference between the appearance of being rich and actually being wealthy. It is abundantly evident that you often see the rich, but you never see the wealthy. To become wealthy, one must embrace stealth wealth. Stealth wealth is about more than just avoiding attention; it's about taking control of your financial temperament while creating a sustainable, secure, and fulfilling life. By living below your means, diversifying your investments, adding value, and avoiding the trappings of wealth, you can achieve financial freedom quicker than most and live life on your own terms. Let's delve deeper into the principles of stealth wealth and explore the strategies and tactics you can use to achieve financial freedom and live a life of abundance. Get ready to embark on a journey to a life of stealth wealth.

PRACTICING STEALTH WEALTH

Stealth wealth is a concept that has become increasingly popular in recent years as people strive to maintain their financial privacy and independence. The idea behind stealth wealth is to live a wealthy lifestyle without advertising it to the world. This can be challenging, as many people feel the urge to show off their financial success, but with a few simple tips, anyone can practice stealth wealth successfully.

Tip 1: Be Honest but Private

One of the key elements of stealth wealth is to be honest about your financial situation but keep the specifics private. When money conversations arise, don't be afraid to share your hopes and fears, but try to avoid giving away too much information. Keep specific numbers and milestones to yourself and only share them with close trusted friends and family members. Understand that most people naturally want to see you doing well to reinforce hope in their lives but never better than them, mainly due to their fear and insecurity. It's never really about you.

Tip 2: Live, but Budget

- Live it up in doses: Stealth wealth is not just about what you say; it's also about how you act. Every high-end purchase or lifestyle upgrade sends a signal to others that you have money to burn, which can lead to complications down the line. To avoid this, steer away from luxurious purchases and focus on living a simple, sustainable lifestyle. This doesn't mean you should deprive yourself of a luxurious life. After all, everything should be in moderation, including moderation itself. But having this mindset of living in doses will not only help you maintain your stealth wealth status but also improve your overall financial well-being and happiness.

- Budgeting: When it comes to budgeting, people who often struggle the most with properly managing their money usually have a hard time tracking their spending. This is why I am a huge advocate of breaking your monthly expenses down to the day. Yes, like the stealth wealthy, it is important to run every financial aspect of your life like a business. Breaking your monthly expenses down to the day enables you to assess your total financial picture and see what your impulsive and toxic spending habits are. There is no need to be ashamed of conducting this budget "stress test." You'll realize that you are not alone regarding frivolous spending. In fact, the average American spends roughly $18,000 a year on non-essential items, along with $300 dollars a month on random and impulsive purchases. Remember, $300 a month saved is just as much as a 7% return on $51,000 invested. In other words, avoiding the infamous "lifestyle creep," saving, and budgeting can be as effective as investing large amounts of your money in most cases.

Tip 3: Focus on Positive Financial Habits

One of the biggest challenges of stealth wealth is the temptation to talk about your financial success. While it's natural to feel proud of your achievements, it's important to avoid the habit of bragging about your wealth. Instead, focus on sharing your financial journey, your habits, and your changing views about money. This allows you to be transparent without advertising your wealth in a way that could cause tension or conflict. Practicing stealth wealth is a mindset shift that takes time and discipline. It's important to remember that stealth wealth is not about hiding your wealth but about living a wealthy life without drawing attention to it. By following these simple tips, you can start living a stealth wealth lifestyle and enjoy the benefits of financial privacy and independence.

Tip 4: Make, Keep, Multiply - Repeat

The stealth wealthy are always looking for ways to have their money produce more of itself. This is the very definition of the name Capital. To them, it's all about the accumulation of assets, and the more assets that are accumulated, the more cash flow you'll have to live off of. So how is this done? Well, for starters, one strategy for multiplying your money is to use the cash flow generated from one asset to purchase another asset that produces additional cash flow.

Here is an example:

1. Buy a Turnkey Useful Business: One way to generate cash flow is to purchase a turnkey useful business. A turnkey business is one that is already established, with a proven track record of success. This type of business can be a great investment opportunity because it allows you to start earning cash flow immediately, without having to build a business from scratch. Businesses such as a turnkey mailbox business, laundromat, or dry cleaning services are resistant to economic contractions in an ordinary business cycle.

2. Use the Cash Flow to Purchase Stocks: Once the turnkey business is generating cash flow, you can use that income to invest in dividend-paying stocks. Dividend-paying stocks are stocks that distribute a portion of their profits to shareholders on a regular basis, providing passive income.

3. Use the Dividend Income to Purchase Real Estate: With the additional income generated from the dividend-paying stocks, you can invest in real estate. Real estate can provide a steady stream of passive income through rental payments, as well as potential appreciation in value over time.

4. Use the Rental Income to Fund Your Lifestyle: As the real estate investment generates rental income, you can use that income to fund your lifestyle or reinvest in additional cash-flowing assets. The goal is to create a cycle of cash flow that allows you

to continue growing your wealth and multiplying your money over time.

Instead of having the asset pay for the liability, have the asset(s) pay for the liability. Meaning, you shouldn't be splurging on expensive liabilities if you haven't accumulated enough assets to utilize the assets' cash flow to do so. Using your hard-earned and working cash is a wasted opportunity to build financial freedom, and it is a sure way to keep you on a never-ending hamster wheel of wealth building. It's also important to note that this strategy requires careful planning, research, and diversification to manage risk effectively. Additionally, it may take a substantial amount of time to build up enough cash flow to make additional investments, so it's important to have a long-term perspective and be patient with the process. Remember, it takes a lifetime to build wealth that lasts lifetimes. It's a marathon, not a sprint.

Tip 5: Ability to Differentiate Value vs. Popular Trends

When it comes to making investment decisions, one must realize that the value of something is not tied to its popularity but to the secondary market for it. Understanding this age-old rule of economics is extremely pivotal to the success rate of investing in anything, and the stealth wealthy know this. They understand that popularity alone does not guarantee value or long-term sustainability. By differentiating value from popularity, investors can avoid the trap of chasing the hype and buying into assets they don't fully understand. This is the number one problem people often face when investing. The allure of quick gains and the fear of missing out can lead to impulsive decisions and potential losses. Instead, investors should focus on their core competencies and stick to what they know. This approach allows them to make informed decisions based on their understanding of the asset and its potential value in the secondary market. By doing so, they can mitigate risks and increase their chances of achieving long-term success.

Ultimately, the ability to differentiate value from popularity is a key factor in successful investing. It requires a thoughtful analysis of the underlying fundamentals and an understanding of market dynamics. By following this principle, investors can navigate the investment landscape with confidence and increase their chances of building wealth over time.

AVOID PAYING TAXES EVEN IN DEATH

In the realm of wealth management, one often encounters the question of whether it is possible to navigate the complex terrain of taxes and protect hard-earned assets for future generations. While the subject may seem daunting, there exists a wealth preservation strategy, a hidden gem cherished by the elite, known as the unified tax credit. Let us unveil this empowering loophole that enables individuals to mitigate the impact of estate taxes, offering a path towards securing a lasting financial legacy.

UNLOCKING THE UNIFIED TAX CREDIT LOOPHOLE:

Picture this: you possess abundant resources, exceeding $675,000 or even $5 million, yet you desire to escape the clutches of the estate tax when the time comes. The unified tax credit is the key to unlocking this seemingly impossible dream. Hidden from popular financial planning advice, this estate tax loophole has long been employed by the stealth wealthy, who skillfully navigate the intricacies of the system. Today, I bring this strategy to light, so that you too may benefit from its transformative potential.

HARNESSING THE POWER OF GIFTING:

Imagine being able to bestow gifts of $14,000 or more annually to your children or grandchildren, without incurring any tax liability. Yes, you read that correctly! The unified tax credit permits you to generously gift as many individuals as you desire, with an annual threshold of $14,000 per recipient. Now, here's the real game-changer: as long as your estate falls below the exemption amount, which is currently set at $675,000, you have the freedom to gift the entirety of your estate, completely tax-free. Astonishingly, in certain scenarios, this loophole even extends to gifting up to $5.75 million, without incurring any federal taxes whatsoever! Prepare to witness the power of the unified tax credit in action.

NAVIGATING POTENTIAL TAX CONSIDERATIONS:

While the unified tax credit presents an exceptional opportunity to reduce your tax burden, it is crucial to be aware of potential tax considerations that may arise for the recipients of your gifts. In particular, beneficiaries may be required to pay taxes on any gains or profits generated from the gifted funds.

For example, if you gift your child $50,000 and they invest it wisely, earning an additional $8,000, they would only be liable to pay taxes on the $8,000. It is worth noting that there is no step-up in basis for these gifted assets, a topic beyond the scope of this discussion. However, it is important to consider the potential tax implications for your beneficiaries when utilizing this strategy.

EMBRACING LONG-TERM WEALTH PRESERVATION:

As we delve deeper into the realm of estate planning, it becomes evident that the unified tax credit offers a compelling alternative to the traditional tax landscape. By utilizing this powerful loophole, you can empower your loved ones to inherit your wealth without the burden of excessive taxation. In contrast, without employing such a strategy, beneficiaries may find themselves subjected to double taxation, as they bear the weight of taxes on both the principal and any gains derived from your estate.

For the stealth wealthy, the choice between preserving wealth and succumbing to the grasp of estate taxes becomes starkly apparent. The unified tax credit represents an extraordinary opportunity to safeguard your hard-earned assets for generations to come. By embracing this knowledge and employing it wisely, you too can join the stealth wealthy mindset of securing a financial legacy that defies the limitations of conventional taxation. Let the unified tax credit be your guiding light, illuminating the path to prosperity and inspiring you to cheat death taxes through strategic planning and empowerment.

TIMELESS HIDDEN WEALTH STRATEGIES

Throughout history, the wealthy have employed various strategies to build their wealth while preserving their privacy. These tactics involve diversifying assets, engaging trusted advisors, and leveraging legal and financial structures. In addition to traditional banks and investments, wealthy individuals explore opportunities in real estate, business ownership, trusts, offshore accounts, and tax-efficient strategies to safeguard and expand their wealth. One effective method employed is the use of trusts, where assets are transferred to trustees on behalf of beneficiaries, providing anonymity and financial growth.

Furthermore, philanthropy and strategic charitable giving serve as dual-purpose approaches to benefit society and minimize public scrutiny. By combining these strategies, the wealthy aim to safeguard their assets, foster wealth growth, and maintain confidentiality in their financial matters. This approach has been utilized by the stealth wealthy, who employ diverse tactics such as asset diversification, seeking reliable advice, and utilizing legal and financial structures like trusts. These strategies ensure wealth protection, privacy maintenance, and thoughtful asset transfer planning.

So, how do these stealth wealth millionaires and billionaires successfully adopt hidden wealth-building strategies?

Let's uncover more of their secrets...

"Would you prefer to earn $1 million once, or $100,000 ten times? The latter embraces the stealthy wealth mindset of building long-term wealth with discretion."

CHAPTER 2:

Understanding the Stealth Wealth Mindset

THE WISDOM QUANT

The wisdom quant, encompassing discernment and equanimity, forms the foundation of the stealth wealthy's investment approach. By exercising discernment, they make informed decisions, divesting themselves of liabilities and focusing on assets that generate wealth. Through equanimity, they remain calm and composed during market fluctuations, maximizing opportunities and effectively managing risk. They are not impulsive or swayed by the latest hype or FOMO (fear of missing out). They often divest themselves of liabilities posing as 'assets' that make them appear to be rich and instead trade them for a sound mind and freedom. In a way, the stealth wealthy, or those who accumulate wealth quietly and maintain a low profile, have a unique approach to investing. Understanding the stealth wealth mindset simply means understanding these core functions of discernment and equanimity that the wealthy use to increase their personal net worth.

Let's find out…

DISCERNMENT AND EQUANIMITY: THE STEALTH WEALTHY'S PATH TO SUCCESSFUL INVESTING

Discernment is the ability to judge well and make wise decisions. Sound judgment is often a tool that requires a blend of common sense and practicality in one's thinking. Discernment is a critical thinking skill for successful investing, and the stealth wealthy are experts in this area. They understand that making wise investment decisions requires careful research and analysis, and they approach investment opportunities with a discerning eye. The stealth wealthy are cautious about taking investment advice from unreliable sources, such as internet fads, social media influencers, or even friends and family who lack financial expertise. Instead, they seek out reliable sources of information, such as reputable financial advisors or respected financial publications.

When evaluating investment opportunities, the stealth wealthy use their discernment to analyze the risks and potential rewards of each opportunity. They carefully consider factors such as the company's financial health, market trends, and economic indicators to determine whether an investment opportunity is worth pursuing. They also take a long-term view of their investments and do not get distracted by short-term fluctuations in the market. They recognize that investing is not a get-rich-quick scheme and that it takes time and patience to achieve long-term wealth creation.

In addition, the stealth wealthy are disciplined and consistent in their investment strategy. They do not let their emotions dictate their investment decisions, and they avoid making impulsive decisions based on fear, greed, or the latest market trend.

By applying discernment to their investments, the stealth wealthy are able to make well-informed decisions that align with their long-term financial goals. They are able to avoid costly mistakes and focus on investment opportunities that have the greatest potential for long-term success. Discernment is an essential skill for successful investing, and the stealth wealthy have mastered this skill through careful research, analysis, and the ability to avoid taking advice from unreliable sources. By using discernment to evaluate investment opportunities and remaining disciplined and consistent in their investment strategy, the stealth wealthy are able to achieve long-term wealth creation and financial success.

THE POWER OF EQUANIMITY IN INVESTING

Equanimity, on the other hand, is the ability to remain calm and composed even in challenging situations. The stealth wealthy apply this skill to their investments by not being swayed by market fluctuations or the emotional reactions of others. They understand that investing is a long-term game, and that short-term fluctuations are just noise. They do not get carried away by euphoria during a bull market or panic during a bear market. Instead, they remain focused on their long-term goals and stick to their investment plan. They also do not let the media or the opinions of friends, influencers, and family influence their investment decisions. Instead, they do their own research and make informed decisions based on facts and data. The stock market is known for its volatility, and there are bound to be ups and downs along the way. Successful investors understand this and do not let their emotions get the best of them during market fluctuations.

The ability to remain calm and composed during challenging situations is what sets the stealth wealthy apart from other investors. One way that the stealth wealthy maintain equanimity is by sticking to their plan. They have a clear understanding of their risk tolerance, investment objectives, and time horizon, and they create a plan that aligns with these factors. This plan serves as a guide for their investment decisions, and they do not deviate from it based on short-term market movements.

The importance of equanimity in investing is not just limited to the stock market. It is also important when it comes to other types of investments, such as real estate or private equity. These investments also have their own set of risks and uncertainties, and successful investors approach them with the same calm and composed mindset. Equanimity is a crucial skill for successful investing and handling the ebbs and flows of life. The ability to remain calm and composed during market fluctuations is what sets the stealth wealthy apart from other investors. By sticking to their investment plan, avoiding emotional reactions, and focusing on their long-term goals, they are able to make informed decisions that lead to long-term wealth creation. Aspiring investors can learn from their example and apply these principles to their own investment strategies.

THE POWER OF MANIFESTATION AND GOAL SETTING

In the realm of building stealth wealth, the power of manifestation and goal setting can be an extraordinary force that propels you towards financial abundance and security. It is an art, a skill, and a mindset that, when mastered, can unlock doors to unimaginable prosperity. Let me paint a powerful message for you, highlighting why sticking to a goal and manifesting is indeed the key to wealth.

In a world driven by instant gratification and short-term gains, those who understand the art of stealth wealth possess a rare gift. They comprehend that true wealth extends far beyond flashy displays and ostentatious symbols of success. Instead, it lies in the profound wisdom of patience, strategic planning, and the unwavering commitment to a long-term vision. Manifestation, the ability to envision your desired financial future, holds incredible power. By harnessing the energy of your thoughts and intentions, you can create a magnetic pull that attracts the very opportunities, resources, and circumstances necessary to realize your goals. It all begins with a crystal-clear vision, an unwavering belief that you are worthy of abundance, and an unyielding determination to make it a reality.

Goal setting, on the other hand, acts as the compass guiding your journey towards wealth. It provides the structure, direction, and milestones needed to measure progress and stay on course. Setting specific, measurable, achievable, relevant, and time-bound (SMART) goals keeps you focused, ensuring that each step you take aligns with your ultimate destination. It helps you break down your grand vision into manageable, actionable steps that can be conquered one by one. Yet, mere goal setting is not enough. The true power lies in your ability to hold onto your goals with unwavering tenacity and resilience. It is the unwavering commitment to your vision, even in the face of adversity or temporary setbacks, that separates those who merely dream from those who manifest their desires. Challenges and obstacles will undoubtedly arise along the path, but it is your ability to rise above them, to adapt and pivot, that will ultimately pave the way to wealth.

Manifestation and goal setting cultivate a mindset that aligns your thoughts, emotions, and actions with your vision. They create a powerful ripple effect, attracting opportunities, connections, and resources that were once unimaginable. By consistently taking inspired action, celebrating even the smallest victories, and persisting when others might give up, you transcend the boundaries of what society deems possible.

Sticking to a goal and manifesting with unwavering faith breeds a resilience that carries you through the highs and lows of your wealth-building journey. It enables you to see beyond immediate gratification, to delay gratification for the sake of long-term rewards. The art of stealth wealth lies in understanding that true riches come not from displaying opulence but from cultivating financial independence, security, and the freedom to live life on your own terms. So, learn to embrace the power of manifestation and goal setting. Paint your vision vividly, set your goals deliberately, and hold them steadfastly. The path to stealth wealth may not always be easy, but as you stay committed to your purpose and manifest your desires, you will unlock a life of abundance, prosperity, and the freedom to design your own destiny.

AVOIDANCE OF FOMO

One of the keys to successful investing is to resist the urge of FOMO. FOMO can cause investors to make irrational decisions based on emotions rather than logic. The stealth wealthy are not immune to FOMO, but they have developed strategies to manage it. They remind themselves that there will always be new investment opportunities and that they do not need to jump on every bandwagon. They also remind themselves of their long-term goals and how impulsive decisions can derail their plans.

The stealth wealthy's approach to investing may not be flashy or exciting, but it is effective. They prioritize long-term gains over short-term wins and avoid impulsive decisions based on FOMO. By practicing discernment and equanimity, they are able to make informed decisions and remain calm during market fluctuations. Aspiring investors can learn from their example and apply these skills to their own investment strategies. Remember, successful investing is not about getting rich quick; it's about building wealth over time.

INVESTING LIKE SYSTEMS RATHER THAN PEOPLE

As stealthy investors, it is important to always be aware of the ever-changing economic landscape and adapt our strategies accordingly. One approach that has proven to be successful during periods of rate hikes and weak economies is focusing on companies with sustainable growth and inelastic demand. Sustainable growth and inelastic demand provide a measure of stability and predictability in the stock market. Companies with a strong track record of sustainable growth and inelastic demand are less likely to be affected by economic fluctuations and are more likely to continue to perform well even in difficult market conditions.

Examples of companies that have demonstrated sustainable growth and inelastic demand include:

1. Utility companies such as Duke Energy, AEP, and American Water.

2. Consumer staples such as Proctor and Gamble, Mondelez, Berkshire Hathaway, and Archer-Daniels-Midland Company.

3. Healthcare companies such as Amgen, United Healthcare, Biogen.

4. Discount retail/Dollar Stores like Dollar General and Costco.

5. Luxury Goods such as LVMH, Ulta Beauty, and Kering.

6. Mega Cap Technology like Microsoft, Apple, Alphabet (Google), Nvidia.

7. Real Estate companies including Realty Income Trust, Blackstone, and LAND.

These companies tend to have steady and predictable revenue streams, and their products or services are not easily replaced by new technology or changing consumer preferences. Another advantage of investing in companies with sustainable growth and inelastic demand is that they can help to mitigate the effects of interest rate hikes. When interest rates rise, it becomes more expensive for companies to borrow money, which can lead to reduced investment and slower growth. However, companies with sustainable growth and inelastic demand are less affected by interest rate hikes, as they have a steady stream of revenue that can support their growth and development.

FOCUS ON THE MOAT

To be the best investor, it's important to identify companies with sustainable growth and inelastic demand. One way to do this is to look for companies that have a strong competitive advantage, such as a unique product or service, a strong brand, or a large market share. These companies are more likely to be able to weather economic downturns and maintain their growth and profitability. One way to identify companies with sustainable growth and inelastic demand is to look for companies that have a strong competitive advantage. A competitive advantage refers to any factor or attribute that allows a company to produce goods or services better or more cheaply than its rivals. Some examples of competitive advantages include:

- A unique product or service: Companies that have developed a unique product or service that is in high demand and not easily replicated by competitors have a strong competitive advantage.

- A strong brand: Companies with a strong brand reputation are more likely to be able to charge premium prices for their products and services and maintain customer loyalty.

- A large market share: Companies that have a large market share in their industry are more likely to be able to weather economic downturns and maintain their growth and profitability.

- Economies of scale: Companies that have a large scale of operations enjoy lower costs of production than their competitors, allowing them to offer their products and services at a lower price and still make a profit.

These are just a few examples of the types of competitive advantages that companies may have. By researching a company's competitive advantages, investors can gain a better understanding of the company's ability to maintain its growth and profitability in difficult market conditions.

Investing in companies with sustainable growth and inelastic demand can provide a measure of stability and predictability in the stock market. One way to identify companies with these characteristics is to look for companies that have a strong competitive advantage. By researching a company's competitive advantages, investors can gain a better understanding of the company's ability to maintain its growth and profitability in difficult market conditions and make informed decisions.

Sustainable growth and inelastic demand are crucial factors that should not be overlooked during periods of rate hikes and weak economies. By focusing on companies with these characteristics, investors can build a portfolio that is not only resilient in the face of market volatility but also has the potential for higher returns and reduced risk.

Note: Remember to always conduct your due diligence and research a company's financials, management, products, and services, and market trends to make informed investment decisions.

THE ART OF CONTRARIAN INVESTING

In a world where following the crowd seems like the safest bet, there is one strategy that revolves around the contrarian approach to investing. By defying conventional wisdom and embracing calculated risks, these financial mavericks have discovered a pathway to extraordinary rewards. Let's delve into the thrilling world of contrarian investing, backed by real-world evidence, and uncover how it can unveil hidden fortunes.

THE CONTRARIAN INVESTOR:

Contrarian investing is all about swimming against the tide of popular opinion and seizing opportunities when others are paralyzed by fear. It requires patience, independent thinking, and a resolute belief in one's analysis. Contrarians understand that market downturns often conceal remarkable prospects for future growth. They are not deterred by short-term fluctuations but rather see them as an entry point to acquire undervalued assets. Take the aftermath of the global financial crisis in 2008 when countless investors were frantically selling off properties. Contrarians, however, recognized the opportunity within the chaos. They swooped in, acquiring distressed assets, and capitalizing on the subsequent recovery. As the market regained its strength, their investments blossomed into significant returns, and their fortunes grew.

Contrarian investing holds the key to unlocking hidden wealth, whether it be stocks, real estate, or any asset class susceptible to market fluctuations. It enables investors to identify hidden gems within the market obscured by prevailing sentiment. While others flock to the trendy and popular, contrarians go off the beaten path, seeking out undervalued assets that have fallen out of favor. These investments may not yield immediate gratification, but the patient contrarian knows that true wealth is cultivated over time. Countless examples exist of stealth billionaires who have thrived by employing the contrarian approach. These individuals are often humble, quietly amassing their fortunes while the world remains fixated on short-term gains. They understand that the contrarian strategy requires discipline, fortitude, and an unwavering belief in their investment theses.

Contrarian investors understand that there isn't always a single right answer or a universally optimal choice. They embrace the idea that different options can lead to different outcomes and that what works for one person may not work for another. This perspective gives them the freedom to explore unconventional strategies and make decisions that deviate from popular opinion. Contrarian thinking allows individuals to break free from societal norms, expectations, and the pressure to conform. It encourages one to critically evaluate their options, consider alternative perspectives, and make decisions based on their values, priorities, and aspirations. Contrarian investors understand that life is short and that it is impossible to experience everything. They embrace the idea that everyone must decide what is most meaningful for them and respect the choices made by others.

BUILDING STEALTH WEALTH
FROM 'FED PIVOTS'

"It's not the pivot that causes the crash. It's usually the event that triggers the pivot."

-JEREMIAH J. BROWN

Usually, when the Federal Reserve enacts a pivot, something broke. A Fed pivot marks the start of a problem in the markets, not the end of them. Following the Fed's 'pivots' has been a way to prepare for recessions and long periods of economic contraction. Historically, every time we've had an inverted yield curve, there has been a recession thereafter, leading to a Fed pivot in hiking the rates. The contrarian investor knows that the Federal Reserve always pivots and adjusts their investment strategy accordingly. This is more about capitalizing on the Fed's pride to keep confidence in the monetary system than it is about data. The main indicator, if the Fed doesn't disclose when they will pivot, will be to follow the yield curve.

WHAT IS A YIELD CURVE?

The yield curve represents the difference between short-term and long-term bond yields and is a major macro-economic gauge in determining the current economic outlook. The curve will invert if short-term bond yields are higher than long-term bond yields. In other words, it would be better to buy a 2-year bond (with a higher yield than the 10-year bond) than it would be to lock your money for 10 years buying a 10-year bond with a lower interest rate since the Fed will probably need to lower rates to stimulate the economy sometime in the future (around that 10-year mark).

REAL ESTATE SHOPPING DURING FED PIVOTS

One example of this is the story of Sam Zell, a billionaire real estate investor who made his fortune by buying up distressed properties during market downturns. In the 1970s, when the real estate market was in a slump, Zell began buying up apartment buildings in cities like Houston and Dallas. By the mid-1980s, he had become one of the largest landlords in the United States, with a portfolio of over 200,000 apartments. He continued to invest in real estate throughout his career, often buying up properties that others had overlooked or deemed too risky. There has also been a recent trend of wealthy investors and institutions such as Blackrock buying up single-family homes and converting them into rental properties. This strategy has become increasingly popular in recent years as low interest rates and high demand for rental properties have created a favorable market for investors. Many of these investors are taking advantage of the current market conditions to buy properties at a discount, with the expectation that they will continue to generate rental income for years to come.

STOCK INVESTMENT DURING FED PIVOTS

The same contrarian approach can be applied to investing in the stock market. During market downturns, when everyone else is selling their stocks, the wealthy often buy. This is because they understand that the stock market is cyclical, and downturns are often followed by periods of growth. One example of this is the story of Warren Buffett, who famously invested in American Express during a period of financial difficulty for the company. He recognized that the company's problems were temporary and that its brand and customer base were strong enough to weather the storm. His investment paid off handsomely, and American Express became one of the most successful invest-ments in his portfolio. Another example is the recent trend of wealthy investors buying shares of companies that have been beaten down by the pandemic. Many of these investors take a long-term approach, buying shares of companies that they believe will rebound as the economy recovers.

HISTORICAL EVIDENCE

Historical evidence also supports the idea that investing in real estate and stocks during times of market downturns can lead to significant long-term wealth. For example, during the Great Depression of the 1930s, many wealthy investors bought up distressed real estate and stocks at bargain prices. Many of these investments went on to generate significant returns over the following decades. The wealthy understand that investing in real estate and stocks during times of market downturns can be a powerful way to generate long-term wealth. While it requires patience and a willingness to take a contrarian approach, the rewards can be significant. By adopting a long-term mindset and investing in assets that have the potential to generate income over time, individuals can create a more stable financial future for themselves and their families.

Hint: Investing in both stocks and real estate during contracting markets can be a lucrative way to build wealth, but it's important to understand the factors that influence market performance during these periods of decline. History has proven that markets often have moments of upward momentum in these down cycles, so don't get caught trying to catch a falling knife. Patience is key in finding the right timing to pull the trigger and buy during these periods. Additionally, market cycles, which occur approximately every ten years, can have a significant impact on the economy and stock market, and the decisions of the Federal Reserve can play a major role in shaping these cycles.

THE POWER OF POLICY-BASED INVESTING

When it comes to the political influence in the world of investing, the wealthiest individuals and families tend to focus on policy, not politics. Rather than making investment decisions based on the latest news headline or political narrative, they take a more systematic approach by analyzing economic data and government policies. By doing so, they can make informed investment decisions that are less susceptible to market volatility and political uncertainty. One recent example of how government policies can impact investments is the California exodus. California has long been known for its high taxes, strict regulations, and overall high cost of living. In 2020, however, the state introduced a new 4% transfer tax on certain properties, which has further incentivized wealthy individuals and families to leave the state.

The California exodus is not unique, and it underscores the importance of policy-based investing. By analyzing government policies and economic data, investors can identify states and regions that offer favorable tax policies, business environments, and other conditions conducive to long-term growth. One of the key benefits of policy-based investing is that it enables investors to minimize risk and maximize returns. By diversifying their portfolios across different asset classes and geographies, they can ensure that their wealth is not tied to any single asset or sector. This can help protect their wealth from market volatility and fluctuations. Another benefit of policy-based investing is that it can help investors stay disciplined and focused on their long-term goals. Rather than making impulsive decisions based on market fluctuations or political narratives, they can make informed decisions based on economic data and government policies. This can help them avoid common investment mistakes, such as trying to time the market or chasing short-term gains.

The data supports the effectiveness of policy-based investing. For example, a study by Morningstar found that investors who focused on low-cost, passively managed index funds outperformed those who invested in actively managed funds over the long term. This is because actively managed funds tend to be more susceptible to market volatility and fluctuations, whereas index funds offer more consistent returns over time.

Policy-based investing is a powerful tool for achieving financial freedom and minimizing risk. By focusing on economic data and government policies, investors can make informed investment decisions that are less susceptible to market volatility and political uncertainty. The

California exodus is just one example of how government policies can impact investments, and policy-based investors are more likely to take this into account. By diversifying their portfolios, staying disciplined, and focusing on their long-term goals, investors can maximize their returns and achieve financial freedom.

The wisdom of discernment and equanimity forms the foundation of the stealth wealthy's investment approach. They make informed decisions by exercising discernment, divesting themselves of liabilities, and focusing on assets that generate wealth. Through equanimity, they remain calm during market fluctuations, effectively managing risk and maximizing opportunities. The stealth wealthy prioritize long-term gains over short-term wins and avoid impulsive decisions driven by FOMO. They invest in companies with sustainable growth and inelastic demand, leveraging their competitive advantages. Furthermore, they embrace contrarian investing, seizing opportunities when others are fearful. By manifesting goals, practicing discernment and equanimity, and adopting contrarian strategies, you, like the stealth wealthy, can master the art of successful investing and wealth accumulation.

"Value EQ over IQ in investing. 80% of investing is behavioral. Not skill. You have to be able to forgo instant gratification and have equanimity if you want to success at long term investing."

CHAPTER 3 :

The Wealth Building Equation - Unveiled

We all have different ideas of what it means to be wealthy. For some, it's owning a fancy car or a big house. For others, it's being able to travel the world or retire early. But what if I told you that true wealth goes beyond material possessions and the desire to "keep up with the Joneses"? True wealth is about having options, the ability to live the life you want without being held back by money. It's about having security, independence, satisfaction, and fulfillment that come from achieving your financial goals.

To achieve true wealth, it is crucial to focus on building your net worth, accumulating assets, managing risks effectively, and ultimately achieving financial freedom. Building your net worth is the first step towards achieving true wealth. Your net worth is the value of all your assets (such as your home, investments, and savings) minus your liabilities (such as your mortgage, car loan, and credit card debt). By increasing the value of your assets and reducing your liabilities, you lay a solid foundation for your financial journey.

ASSET ACCUMULATION

Accumulating assets is another key aspect of achieving true wealth. Investing in assets that generate income, such as rental properties or dividend-paying stocks, provides a steady stream of revenue that can help you achieve financial freedom. Diversifying your income streams not only provides security and independence but also protects against potential market volatility.

Financial freedom is the ultimate goal of building your net worth and accumulating assets. It means having enough income to cover your living expenses without having to work actively. Financial freedom allows you to live life on your terms and pursue your passions and interests without being constrained by financial limitations.

While building net worth, accumulating assets, and achieving financial freedom may seem challenging, it doesn't have to be overwhelming. You don't need to be a millionaire or retire early to start your journey towards true wealth. It's all about taking small steps, making smart financial decisions, and being persistent. Begin by creating a budget and sticking to it. Saving a portion of your income and investing it wisely, even in low-cost index funds, can make a significant impact over time. Paying off debts helps decrease liabilities and increase your net worth. Exploring additional income-generating opportunities, such as renting out a room or freelancing, can boost your overall financial stability.

Remember, true wealth transcends material possessions and societal comparisons. It lies in financial freedom, security, independence, and personal fulfillment. By building your net worth, accumulating assets, and achieving financial freedom through thoughtful planning and perseverance, you can attain true wealth.

THE RULE OF 33%

The traditional 60/40 diversification split has long hindered the average person's ability to build and multiply their wealth. It's no wonder that, based on actual data, the top 0.01 percent own more wealth than the bottom 99% of the population. This investment philosophy has fostered uneven diversification, overexposing investors to concentrated risks due to a limited number of investments, leaving their portfolios vulnerable to the performance of a few assets or sectors. It also underexposes them to investments across multiple asset classes, making significant growth difficult to achieve. However, there is one rule that the stealth wealthy have been following since even before this century—the Rule of 33%.

The "Rule of 33%" is an investment principle that suggests diversifying one's wealth into three equal parts:

1. One-third in land.

2. One-third in business.

3. One-third in 'liquid' assets.

This principle is often attributed to the Talmud, a central text of Jewish law and teachings. While the Talmud provides guidance on financial matters, it does not specifically mention the Rule of 33% or tie it to the wealth-building practices of the Jewish population. However, the Rule of 33% still offers a useful framework for diversifying investments. Diversification is widely recognized as a fundamental strategy for managing investment risk and maximizing potential returns.

For layman investors, applying the Rule of 33% to their investment strategy involves allocating their wealth across three main categories: land, business, and liquid assets. Here's how this can be executed:

1. Land: Investing in land can include purchasing residential or commercial properties, investing in real estate investment trusts (REITs), or acquiring land for development. Land investments can provide long-term appreciation potential, rental income, or opportunities for property development. Consider factors such as location, market trends, and potential rental demand when making land-related investment decisions.

2. Business: Investing in businesses can range from owning shares in publicly traded companies to starting or acquiring private ventures. For the everyday stealth investor, a common approach is to invest in stocks through the stock market. Research and analyze companies across different industries, focusing on their financial health, growth potential, and competitive advantages. Alternatively, investing in exchange-traded funds (ETFs) or mutual funds can offer diversification within the business category.

3. Liquid Assets: Liquid assets refer to readily available cash or investments that can be easily converted into cash. This category includes bank accounts, money market funds, stocks, bonds, and other highly liquid investments. Layman investors can consider building an emergency fund to cover unexpected expenses and allocate a portion of their portfolio to stocks and bonds based on their risk tolerance and investment goals.

When applying the Rule of 33%, it's important to consider your individual financial situation, risk tolerance, and investment objectives. Here are a few key considerations for executing this strategy effectively:

- Portfolio allocation: Divide your investment portfolio roughly equally into land, business, and liquid assets. Adjust the allocation based on your risk appetite, investment knowledge, and market conditions.

- Diversify within each category: Within each segment, further diversify your investments to reduce risk. For example, in the business category, invest in companies from various sectors and sizes to spread the risk.

- Periodic review: Regularly assess and rebalance your portfolio to ensure your allocation remains in line with your investment strategy. Market conditions and personal circumstances may warrant adjustments to maintain diversification.

It's important to note that the Rule of 33% is not a one-size-fits-all approach, and individual circumstances may require deviations or modifications to suit personal goals and risk preferences. Consulting with a financial advisor or investment professional can provide valuable guidance and help tailor the strategy to your specific needs. The stealth wealthy investor can apply the Rule of 33% by diversifying their wealth across land, business, and liquid assets. By allocating investments across these categories, they can reduce risk and potentially maximize returns. Remember to conduct thorough research, regularly review and adjust your portfolio, and seek professional advice as needed to align your investment strategy with your financial goals.

THE POWER OF THE DETAILS: MASTERY IN INVESTING

In the realm of investing, there exists a breed of individuals known as stealth wealth masters who have mastered the art of wealth accumulation through their addiction to the details. These individuals understand that investing requires careful analysis, research, and constant monitoring.

Becoming a stealth wealth master entails grasping the importance of understanding your income sources and meticulously examining expenses. By tracking spending habits and identifying areas to reduce costs, you can redirect those funds towards building your investment portfolio. Immersing yourself in finance and constantly researching market trends and investment opportunities becomes second nature. Focusing on understanding the fundamentals of potential investments, analyzing risks and rewards, and actively managing and minimizing debt become essential practices.

For the stealth wealthy, true wealth and financial security are not just about making money. They recognize that wealth accumulation goes hand in hand with effectively managing risks. Thorough risk assessments are an integral part of their journey towards financial prosperity. They stay informed about emerging trends, economic indicators, and geopolitical factors that can impact their investments. By staying ahead of the curve, they make informed decisions and mitigate potential risks.

Diversification serves as a cornerstone of the stealth wealthy's risk management strategy. They understand the importance of spreading investments across various asset classes, such as stocks, bonds, real estate, and commodities. Within each asset class, further diversification by allocating funds to different sectors and geographic regions minimizes vulnerability. Striking a balance between high-risk, high-reward investments and stable, income-generating assets helps manage exposure to volatility and aligns with long-term objectives.

Thorough risk assessments and due diligence are routine practices for the stealth wealthy. They carefully weigh potential risks and rewards by analyzing financial statements, assessing industry trends, and evaluating management teams' track records. This meticulous research empowers them to make informed decisions and identify potential pitfalls before committing their resources.

The stealth wealthy also employ proactive risk mitigation strategies. While they acknowledge that risk cannot be completely eliminated, they implement techniques such as hedging through options and futures contracts to offset potential losses. Implementing stop-loss orders helps limit downside risk. Regularly reviewing and rebalancing portfolios ensures a disciplined approach to maintaining a favorable risk exposure.

The journey to true wealth and financial security may seem challenging, but with perseverance, education, and dedication to managing risks effectively, the stealth wealthy pave the way for a secure financial future. By incorporating these principles into your own financial journey, you too can achieve true wealth and build a foundation of financial security.

THE IMPORTANCE OF EXCLUSIVITY

When it comes to achieving stealth wealth, exclusivity is key. The stealth wealthy is not interested in making the same investments as everyone else. Instead, they look for opportunities that are unique and have the potential for greater returns. For example, while the majority of people may be focused on investing in the stock market or buying expensive properties in highly sought-after neighborhoods, the stealth wealthy may instead choose to invest in undervalued real estate in up-and-coming areas or in small businesses with high growth potential and purchase these undervalued assets using a LOC against their more trophy or prime assets. By going against the crowd and making these exclusive and quiet investments, the person is able to achieve greater returns and build wealth more efficiently.

> *"Why would you care that you're
> not where everyone is? Exclusivity
> is being everywhere no one is."*
>
> **-UNKNOWN**

Additionally, the concept of exclusivity goes beyond just investment opportunities. The stealth wealthy also prioritizes privacy and discretion in their financial decisions and actions. They may choose to keep their wealth a secret from friends and family, and may avoid flashy and extravagant purchases that would draw attention to their wealth. One example of this exclusivity in action is the use of offshore bank accounts and trusts. While these financial tools can be controversial, they can also provide a level of financial privacy and asset protection that is not available through traditional banking methods. By utilizing these exclusive financial tools, the stealth wealthy is able to keep their wealth and financial decisions private.

It's important to note that achieving stealth wealth is not about being secretive or unethical. It's about making smart financial decisions and being strategic in how you manage and grow your wealth. By focusing on exclusivity, the stealth wealthy is able to build wealth more efficiently and effectively, without drawing unwanted attention to themselves. However, it's crucial to be aware of the legal aspects and regulations surrounding the use of offshore bank accounts and trusts. It's important to consult with a financial advisor or attorney to ensure that the use of these financial tools is compliant with the laws and regulations in the country of residence. Exclusivity, applies to one's lifestyle choices. The stealth wealthy may choose to live in a modest home, drive a used car, and wear inexpensive clothing, but indulge in the business of buying assets and, increasing ones networth.

TRUE WEALTH IS REVEALED IN WHAT YOU DON'T SEE

Stealth wealth is the practice of making positive progress on your finances while drawing as little attention to that progress as possible, in order to avoid uncomfortable situations and interpersonal tensions that may arise when others perceive one as "wealthy" or wealthier than them. The goal of stealth wealth is to maintain one's financial goals without sacrificing their relationships and mental health. It typically involves not bringing up financial numbers or details with others, save for a few trusted loved ones, setting up proper shell companies to conceal asset holdings, and being discreet and private rather than secretive.

HIDE IT UNDER A MATTRESS OR IN A SHELL?

The Panama Papers refer to a massive leak of financial and legal documents from the Panamanian law firm Mossack Fonseca in April 2016. The documents revealed the ways in which wealthy individuals and companies used offshore shell companies to conceal their assets and avoid taxes. The papers showed that Mossack Fonseca had helped set up more than 214,000 shell companies for clients around the world. These shell companies were then used to open bank accounts, purchase property, and conduct business transactions, all while obscuring the true ownership of the assets in question.

One common method of hiding wealth in the Panama Papers was through the use of anonymous shell companies. These are companies that exist only on paper and have no real operations or employees. They are often registered in tax havens, where financial regulations are lax and secrecy is guaranteed. There are several tax havens around the world that are known for having lax financial regulations and strong secrecy laws. Some of the most popular jurisdictions for setting up offshore shell companies include:

1. Panama: The country from which the Panama Papers leak originated, Panama is known for its strict banking secrecy laws and its ability to provide anonymous incorporation services.

2. The British Virgin Islands: This British Overseas Territory is a popular destination for incorporating offshore companies because of its low corporate tax rates and its reputation as a business-friendly jurisdiction.

3. The Seychelles: This island nation in the Indian Ocean is known for its low incorporation costs and easy registration process for offshore companies.

4. The Bahamas: This island nation is a popular destination for incorporating offshore companies because of its low taxes and its reputation as a business-friendly jurisdiction.

5. Belize : This Central American country is known for its low incorporation costs and easy registration process for offshore companies.

By transferring assets into these companies, wealthy individuals and companies were able to conceal their ownership of the assets and avoid taxes in their home countries.

Another way to hide wealth was to use nominees, people who front as the owner of the assets while the true owner keep hidden. By using nominees, wealthy individuals and companies could maintain control over their assets while keeping their identities secret. For example, the true owner of the assets might transfer ownership of the assets to the offshore shell company, and then use nominees to sign documents and make decisions on behalf of the company. The nominee directors and officers would be listed on the company's incorporation papers and other official documents, and they would be the ones who would appear in public records as the owners of the assets. But in reality, the true owner would be the one making the decisions and calling the shots.

Another way to use nominees is to appoint them as trustees of a trust, which is a legal arrangement where assets are held and managed by one or more trustees for the benefit of one or more beneficiaries. Trusts can be set up to hold various types of assets, such as bank accounts, real estate, and investments. The nominee trustees would be listed as the legal owners of the assets, but the true owner would be the one directing the trustees on how to manage the assets.

It's important to note that in many countries, it is illegal to use nominees in this way to conceal assets or avoid taxes.

It's also worth mentioning that some countries and financial institutions are implementing KYC(Know your customer) and AML (anti-money laundering) regulations, making it harder to use nominees, As these regulations require the financial institutions to know who the true beneficial owner of the assets are. As always, It's always recommended to consult with legal and financial advisor before trying to conceal and protect wealth, as it could bring legal and financial consequences depending on the jurisdiction and specific circumstances.

OFFSHORE IT

To set up an offshore shell company in one of these jurisdictions, an individual or company typically hires a law firm or incorporation agent that specializes in setting up such companies. The process typically involves the following steps:

1. Choose a jurisdiction: Decide where you want to incorporate your offshore company.

2. Select a company name: Choose a name for your company that is available and complies with the jurisdiction's requirements.

3. File incorporation papers: Prepare and file the necessary incorporation papers, such as the articles of incorporation, with the relevant government authority.

4. Obtain an EIN (Employer Identification Number): or a Tax ID number

5. Appoint directors and officers: Appoint directors and officers for the company. These people may be nominees that front for the true owner of the assets.

6. Obtain a registered agent and/or office: Most jurisdictions require an offshore company to have a registered agent and/or office within the country. These are usually provided by the law firm or incorporation agent you hire.

Keep in mind that some of these steps may vary depending on the jurisdiction, and some of these jurisdictions are becoming more transparent and some actions could be considered illegal and/or involve penalties. Additionally, it's important to note that creating offshore shell companies for the purpose of avoiding taxes or hiding assets may be illegal in some countries, depending on the jurisdiction and the specific circumstances.

The concept of stealth wealth is motivated by the goal of avoiding uncomfortable situations that can arise when the people around you view you as "wealthy". *Stealth wealth is a term used to describe a lifestyle in which individuals maintain a low public profile of their financial success, choosing to live simply and avoid conspicuous consumption. It is characterized by a focus on saving and investing, rather than spending and showing off wealth.

BUYING MONEY: THE OWNERSHIP OF CAPITAL

In the realm of the stealth wealthy, the concept of money takes on a different meaning. "Money is too valuable to spend," a statement attributed to an unknown billionaire, encapsulates their mindset. These individuals have a common trait regardless of their industry: they all own capital. As their wealth increases, their income relies less on labor and more on capital. In fact, over 70% of their earnings stem from capital, whereas the average employee's income is predominantly derived from labor. The reason behind the rich getting richer lies in their ownership of capital, which offers favorable tax advantages.

UNDERSTANDING CAPITAL:

But what exactly is capital? It is simply anything you own that can generate income for you. Examples of capital include investment properties, stocks, intellectual property, businesses, your personal likeness or popularity, and patents, trademarks, and copyrights. Capital ownership opens up a range of possibilities, such as renting out your assets, licensing them for others to use, selling them for a profit, using them as collateral for borrowing capital, passing them down to loved ones, or even building upon them to create more assets.

THE POWER OF OWNERSHIP:

At the heart of this discussion is the concept of ownership, particularly owning capital that can generate income. Building a billion-dollar fortune solely through regular employment and paying standard income tax rates is highly unlikely. The prevailing trend, as observed, is that owning capital is more advantageous than laboring for it, a fact even reflected in the tax code. In this age where capital ownership leads to wealth, relying solely on labor as a long-term strategy may not be prudent. It is important to note that the labor force has always been the driving force of innovation and productivity, and it is hoped that this dynamic will continue. However, in an era marked by automation, globalization, and financialization, the opportunity to accumulate wealth without manual labor has shifted in favor of capital owners rather than workers.

MONEY MAKES MONEY:

The adage "money never sleeps" perfectly aligns with the idea of capital ownership. This is because the rate of return on capital tends to outpace the overall economic growth rate. On average, the return on capital ranges from 5% to 7%, whereas the growth rate of the economy hovers around 2% to 3%. This disparity enables inheritors of wealth and capital owners to maintain their desired lifestyle while their accumulated capital continues to outpace the economy. Consequently, a persistent wealth and income divide emerges within societies. Merely working hard for fiat money without converting it into income-generating assets can be seen as financial suicide. It is akin to holding your breath underwater – you may survive for a while, but eventually, you will run out of air. Unfortunately, the structure of our system is designed to favor capital holders.

BUYING AND CREATING CASH FLOW: A PATH TO WEALTH

Building wealth through cash flow is a key principle embraced by the stealth wealthy. While it may seem like a concept reserved for the ultra-rich, ordinary investors can also adopt strategies to generate consistent cash flow and accumulate wealth over time. By focusing on practical approaches, individuals can leverage their resources and investments to create passive income streams, just like the stealth wealthy do. Similarly to buying a new TV, car, or even spending thousands on concert tickets, investing in companies that engage in mass discretionary consumer spending and pay dividends could be a strategy to help you generate cash flow from your capital.

Moreover, if you possess creative talents or intellectual property, you can monetize them by licensing or selling them for royalties. This includes music, books, artwork, software, patents, or trademarks. By leveraging your creative assets, you can earn passive income as others pay to use or access your work. Collaborate with professionals in respective industries to explore licensing agreements, publishing deals, or partnerships that can generate ongoing cash flow. As you continue to evolve in buying or creating cash flow from either your physical or intellectual capital, you'll soon realize that capital's true purpose is to make more of itself through the form of cash flow.

Understanding the power of capital ownership is essential for aspiring wealth creators. Billionaires have unlocked the gateway to prosperity by shifting their focus from labor to capital ownership.

Owning assets that generate income provides long-term financial security and allows for exponential wealth growth. By embracing the concept of buying cash flow, such as through retail triple net and industrial triple net leases, individuals can harness the potential of their capital and pave their way to financial freedom.

> **"If investing is entertaining and you're having fun, you're probably not investing but gambling."**

CHAPTER 4: THE BUSINESS OF BORING

Today, it seems that many people are agnostic when it comes to valuations. They prefer quick returns from day trading or making short-term bets on the next new trend by leveraging up their investments. In a world of quantitative easing, speculation, and growth bubbles, the idea of investing in "boring" companies may seem unattractive and outdated to many investors. However, for the stealth wealthy, it is a tried and true method of earning millions off of value-based investments and stocks.

Fun Fact: Did you know that over the last 80 years, 80% of the market's returns came from dividends, not capital appreciation?

IDENTIFYING VALUE-BASED COMPANIES

The term "business of boring" refers to investing in companies that may not have the hype and excitement of new technology startups or hot industries, but have consistent profitability and stable growth. These companies often operate in industries that are inelastic, meaning that demand for their products or services remains relatively stable regardless of economic conditions. One prime example of a company in the business of boring is Dollar General. With over 17,000 stores across 46 states, Dollar General is a mega-cap company that has seen steady growth over the years. Its business model of offering affordable products to lower-income consumers has proven to be resilient during economic downturns, as people still need to buy basic necessities even when times are tough. Another example is Procter & Gamble, a consumer goods company that owns household names like Tide, Pampers, and Crest. These products are necessities that people will continue to buy, regardless of the economic climate. As a result, Procter & Gamble has seen consistent growth and has been a reliable investment for decades. Other mega-cap companies in the business of boring include Coca-Cola, Amgen, Lockheed Martin, McDonald's, and Walmart. These companies may not be the flashiest or most exciting investments, but they have proven to be resilient and profitable over the years.

The key to success in the business of boring is identifying companies with strong fundamentals, such as a history of consistent earnings growth, strong cash flow with dividends, and a sustainable competitive advantage. These companies may not have the same level of hype as new technology startups, but they provide a stable foundation for a well-diversified investment portfolio.

Innovation is also important in the business of boring. Companies that can adapt to changing consumer preferences and technological advancements are more likely to thrive in the long run. For example, Dollar General has embraced e-commerce and mobile payments to stay competitive with larger retailers, while Procter & Gamble has invested in sustainability initiatives to appeal to environmentally conscious consumers. The business of boring may not be the most exciting investment strategy, but it can provide consistent and reliable returns for those willing to take a long-term view. Mega-cap companies with a history of strong fundamentals and innovation are the safest bets, and companies like Dollar General, Berkshire Hathaway, Exxon Mobile, Lockheed Martin, and Procter & Gamble are likely to be here forever. By focusing on value-based investments and stocks, the stealth wealthy can earn millions while avoiding the speculative bubbles and risks that come with trend-chasing.

CASHFLOW FIRST, FOLLOWED BY APPRECIATION

When it comes to building wealth, there are various strategies that one can employ. Some investors prioritize growth, while others focus on value or income. However, there is a growing consensus among experts and the stealth wealthy that the most effective way to build long-term wealth is through a cashflow-first approach. The idea behind a cashflow-first approach is simple: prioritize investments that generate consistent, reliable income streams. This might include dividend-paying stocks, rental properties, or bonds. By focusing on cashflow, investors can build a stable financial foundation that can weather market downturns and provide a reliable source of income throughout their lives.

WHY IS CASH FLOW SO IMPORTANT?

For one, it provides a cushion against volatility. When the stock market drops or real estate values decline, investors who rely solely on growth or appreciation can find themselves in a precarious position. Without a reliable source of income, they may be forced to sell their investments at a loss or dip into savings to cover expenses. By contrast, investors who prioritize cash flow can weather market downturns without having to sell their assets, allowing them to hold on until values recover.

Another advantage of a cash flow-first approach is that it can help investors achieve financial freedom earlier in life. By generating enough passive income to cover living expenses, investors can choose to retire or pursue other interests without relying on a traditional job or the future growth and appreciation of the asset itself. This can be a powerful motivator for those who aspire to achieve financial independence and live life on their own terms without worry.

Of course, this doesn't mean that appreciation isn't important. In fact, appreciation can be a powerful source of long-term wealth creation. By investing in assets with potential value growth over time, investors can generate significant returns that compound over decades. However, the key is to view appreciation as the icing on the cake rather than the main course. By prioritizing cash flow first and foremost, investors can build a stable and reliable financial foundation that allows them to seize appreciation opportunities as they arise.

SO, WHAT DOES IT TAKE TO ADOPT A CASH FLOW-FIRST MINDSET?

Firstly, it requires a willingness to prioritize income over growth or speculation. This may involve foregoing high-flying tech stocks in favor of dividend-paying stalwarts or choosing to invest in real estate rather than cryptocurrency. It also demands discipline and patience, as income-oriented investments may not always produce the eye-popping returns of their growth-oriented counterparts. Ultimately, the cash flow-first approach is a powerful tool for building long-term wealth. By focusing on generating reliable income streams, investors can establish a stable financial foundation capable of weathering market turbulence and providing a source of passive income throughout their lives. With appreciation serving as the icing on the cake, investors can enjoy the benefits of both income and growth as they steadily build their wealth over time.

HOW TO VALUE ANY INVESTMENT

In essence, all investments come down to cash flow and the predictability of that cash flow. Cash flow and its predictability are crucial factors to consider when evaluating any investment. Cash flow refers to the amount of cash or cash-equivalent that an investment generates over a specific time period, while predictability of cash flow refers to the level of certainty or uncertainty associated with the timing and amount of the cash flow.

To evaluate the predictability of an investment, several methods can be employed:

1. Financial Statement Analysis: One way to assess the predictability of an investment is by analyzing the company's financial statements. By examining the income statement, balance sheet, and cash flow statement, investors can gain a better understanding of the company's financial performance over time.

2. Historical Performance: Another method is to evaluate the investment's historical performance. Investments that have demonstrated consistent performance over time may be considered more predictable than those with volatile performance.

3. Analysis of Management Team and Industry: The management team and the industry in which the company operates can also provide insights into the predictability of the investment. Companies with strong, experienced management teams operating in stable industries tend to be more predictable than those with weaker management teams or operating in volatile industries.

4. Financial Metrics: Various financial metrics such as cash flow from operations (CFO), free cash flow (FCF), return on investment (ROI), gross profit margin, and net profit margin can indicate the predictability of cash flow and performance. Companies with high and consistent CFO, FCF, ROI, and margins may be considered more predictable than those with lower and inconsistent metrics.

5. Financial Ratio Analysis: Conducting an analysis of financial ratios such as debt-to-equity ratio and current ratio can evaluate a company's ability to service its debt and its liquidity. This assessment can provide insights into the predictability of future cash flows and determine the company's level of indebtedness compared to its cash reserves.

The stealthy wealthy investor has takes it a step further to cut through the clutter and identify great company stock to invest in. Let's explore their methodology step by step, providing you with the tools to analyze companies beyond just reading their 10-K statements.

1. Start with GDP Growth: The Rising Tide

To gauge the macroeconomic state of businesses, the first step is to examine the GDP growth. This rising tide of the economy sets the foundation for companies to thrive. Look for countries or regions with strong GDP growth as they tend to create a favorable environment for businesses to flourish.

2. Focus on Growing Free Cash Flow

Free cash flow is a critical indicator of a company's financial health. It represents the cash left over after deducting capital expenditures from operating cash flow. Identify companies that demonstrate consistent growth in free cash flow. This indicates their ability to generate cash from their operations and reinvest in their business.

3. Seek Understandable Business Models with Clear Revenue Paths

Simplicity is key when it comes to successful investing. Look for companies with understandable business models and clear paths to revenue generation. These straightforward deals provide the foundation for financial abundance in investing.

4. Assessing Companies with Strong Economic Moats

Utilize financial platforms like MSN Money or Morningstar to identify companies with strong economic moats, also known as competitive advantages. These moats protect companies from competitors and contribute to their long-term success. Once you've identified a company with a strong economic moat, move on to the following criteria for analysis.

INCOME STATEMENT:

- Goal: Net Income should always be positive. This indicates that the company is generating more revenue than expenses.

BALANCE SHEET:

- Goal: Net Equity should always be positive. This represents the difference between a company's assets and liabilities.

CASH FLOW STATEMENT:

- Operating Net Cash Flow: Aim for a positive value, indicating the company's ability to generate cash from its operations.

- Investment Activities: Negative values indicate that the company is reinvesting capital gains back into itself.

- Financing Activities: Negative values indicate that the company is either buying back shares, increasing stock prices, or distributing dividends to shareholders.

Consider the analysis and ratings provided by analysts as an additional input for your evaluation. Pay attention to the following metrics:

- Price to Earnings (P/E) Ratio: Determine if the stock or company is overvalued. The stealthy wealthy investor's strategy is to aim for a P/E ratio no higher than 18 times the company's annual earnings.

- Price to Book (P/B) Ratio: Evaluate the real value or book value of the stock or company. The ideal P/B ratio is no more than 2 times the book value.

- Debt to Equity Ratio: Measure the riskiness of a company by comparing its debt to the amount of equity it holds. A debt to equity ratio of 0.40 or lower is considered an ideal metric, indicating vigilant leadership.

- Current Ratio: Assess whether a company's liquid assets are greater than its liabilities. The strategy is to look for a current ratio of at least 1.5, which ensures that assets are at least twice as big as liabilities.

For a more comprehensive analysis, consider the following advanced metrics:

- Margin of Safety: Calculated as the Book Value divided by the Share Price, this metric provides an indication of the safety of an investment. The closer the equity is to the market price, the safer the investment.

- Competitive Advantage or Economic Moat: Evaluate the company's gross profit margin as an indicator of its economic viability and moat.

- Gross Profit Margin Assessment:

- 35% and under: Indicates low dominance in the industry.

- 35% - 50%: Suggests medium dominance.

- 50% or more: Implies high dominance in the industry.

By applying these analytical techniques and metrics, you can gain a deeper understanding of a company's financial health, competitive position, and potential for long-term success. Remember, simplicity, solid fundamentals, and a focus on free cash flow are the keys to achieving financial abundance in your investment journey. It is important to note that relying on a single metric alone cannot provide a complete understanding of an investment's predictability. Instead, investors should employ a combination of these methods, analyzing multiple data points to gain a comprehensive understanding of the investment's predictability.

Stealth wealthy Investors generally prefer investments with stable and predictable cash flows as they allow for better planning of future financial needs and objectives. Additionally, for an investment to be attractive, it should generate sufficient cash flow to provide returns to investors and support future growth and reinvestment if necessary. While cash flow and predictability are critical considerations, they should not be the sole factors in making investment decisions.

BEWARE OF ZOMBIE COMPANIES

In addition to these fundamental analysis techniques, investors must be cautious of the rise of "zombie companies" that primarily rely on stimulus and debt to survive. Zombie companies, as defined by the Bank of International Settlements, are companies that cannot generate enough profits to cover the interest on their debt and are sustained through low-interest rates and deregulation. In recent years, the number of zombie companies has reached record highs, with nearly 10% of listed non-financial firms in advanced economies fitting this definition. Such companies pose significant risks to investors, as they are highly vulnerable to default when interest rates rise or the stimulus ends.

To avoid investing in companies reliant on stimulus and debt for survival, investors should closely examine a company's dependence on government support and debt. A company heavily reliant on government stimulus and debt to sustain its operations is likely to be a poor investment choice. Investors should pay attention to indicators such as the debt-to-equity ratio and interest coverage ratio. High debt-to-equity ratios and low interest coverage ratios indicate heavy reliance on debt. Furthermore, investors should consider a company's revenue and profitability. Companies with weak revenue and consistent losses are likely to be unfavorable investments. By focusing on fundamental factors such as free cash flow, economic moat, and financial statements, investors can identify strong companies and minimize the risk of investing in overvalued or risky stocks. Being aware of the rise of zombie companies, which can only survive due to low interest rates and easy access to debt, helps investors avoid companies with unsustainable business models. Successful investing requires careful analysis and a long-term perspective. It is important to focus on a company's underlying fundamentals and avoid getting swayed by short-term trends or hype. With a disciplined approach to investing, investors can achieve their financial goals and build long-term wealth.

HOW TO ANALYZE BULLET-PROOF INVESTMENT PROPERTIES

In the realm of real estate investing, the ultimate goal for many stealthy investors is to find properties that generate substantial cash flow while maintaining a low profile. One effective approach to achieving this is through the use of Debt Service Coverage Ratio (DSCR) loans. DSCR loans are commercial real estate loans that consider the Debt Service Coverage Ratio as a key factor in determining the borrower's eligibility. These loans, often referred to as "agency debt" loans, assess the property's income to qualify for financing rather than relying solely on the borrower's creditworthiness. In this type of loan, the bank prioritizes the performance of the property over the borrower's personal circumstances. The DSCR loan calculates the property's debt service coverage ratio by dividing the net operating income (NOI) by the annual debt service.

For example: $100,000 (Net Operating Income) / $130,000 (Annual Loan Amount) = 1.3 DSCR

If the ratio meets the lender's requirements (usually 1.2 DSCR or higher), the borrower can secure financing for the property, indicating official credit approval for the deal. Lenders rarely rely on your personal ability to repay the loan if the property's income can cover it.

WHY ARE DSCR LOANS BENEFICIAL?

DSCR loans offer several advantages for stealth investors. One major benefit is that these loans are based on the property's cash flow rather than the borrower's creditworthiness. As long as the property generates enough income to cover the debt service, the loan is approved. Lenders typically care less about your personal credit in this scenario. This is advantageous for stealth investors who aim to maintain a low profile and avoid drawing attention to their creditworthiness. Additionally, DSCR loans enable investors to acquire properties with a lower down payment compared to traditional commercial real estate loans, which usually require a down payment of 20-30%. In contrast, DSCR loans may allow borrowers to put down as little as 10%, facilitating the acquisition of multiple properties with less capital and making it easier to diversify their portfolio.

When using DSCR loans to analyze investment properties, the initial step is to calculate the property's debt service coverage ratio by dividing the net operating income by the annual debt service. Most lenders require a ratio of at least 1.25 to qualify for a DSCR loan. However, stealth investors should aim for a ratio of 1.5 or higher to ensure that the property generates enough cash flow to cover unexpected expenses or periods of vacancy. Another crucial factor to consider when analyzing investment properties with DSCR loans is the property's location and growth potential. Stealth investors should focus on areas with high rental demand, low vacancy rates, and strong economic growth prospects. It is also important to assess the property's potential for appreciation and whether the rental income is likely to increase in the future.

DSCR loans serve as an effective tool for stealth investors seeking to analyze and acquire bullet-proof investment properties. These loans allow investors to qualify for financing based on the property's cash flow rather than their creditworthiness, facilitating a low-profile approach. When analyzing investment properties with DSCR loans, it is essential to calculate the debt service coverage ratio and focus on properties with strong cash flow potential and promising growth prospects. By adhering to these guidelines, stealth investors can build a profitable real estate portfolio while maintaining a low profile.

HOUSE HACKING: WEALTH THROUGH STRATEGIC REAL ESTATE INVESTMENT

"If you live like no one else would today, you could own what no one else can tomorrow."

-JEREMIAH J BROWN

There are many ways to build wealth outside of analyzing cash flow. In the realm of the everyday investor looking to build wealth in stealth, house hacking can be your ticket to doing so. House hacking has emerged as a powerful strategy that allows individuals to generate income and build equity through real estate while simultaneously enjoying the benefits of homeownership. Apart from the financial advantages, house hacking can also be a tool for stealth wealth, providing individuals with the opportunity to grow their net worth discreetly. Sacrificing creature comforts from more prestigious turnkey homes and putting sweat equity into building out a turnkey home for others can significantly improve one's net worth and force equity appreciation unlike anything else in real estate. Moreover, there are tax exemptions associated with staying in a residence for a specific period, presenting additional incentives for those pursuing house hacking as a wealth-building approach.

UNDERSTANDING HOUSE HACKING

House hacking involves the strategic acquisition of a property with the intention of offsetting or eliminating living expenses by generating rental income from portions of the property. This strategy typically involves purchasing a multi-unit property, such as a duplex, triplex, or fourplex, living in one unit, and renting out the remaining units to cover a significant portion, if not all, of the mortgage and other expenses.

BUILDING WEALTH THROUGH HOUSE HACKING

House hacking enables individuals to significantly reduce or eliminate their housing expenses by having tenants cover a substantial portion of the mortgage, property taxes, and other costs associated with homeownership. As tenants pay rent, the house hacker can use the generated income to build equity in the property. Over time, this equity growth can be leveraged for future real estate investments or other wealth-building opportunities. Not to mention, real estate, historically, has demonstrated the potential for long-term appreciation. By strategically selecting and managing properties, house hackers can benefit from property value appreciation, contributing to their overall wealth accumulation. House hacking also allows individuals to build wealth more discreetly than other investment strategies. Unlike flashy luxury purchases or conspicuous displays of wealth, real estate investments can remain hidden from prying eyes, providing a level of privacy and security.

TWO-YEAR RESIDENCE RULE:

The Internal Revenue Service (IRS) offers tax benefits to homeowners who have lived in their primary residence for at least two out of the past five years. This rule allows married couples to exclude up to $500,000 of capital gains from the sale of their home, while single individuals can exclude up to $250,000. These tax exemptions can be a significant advantage for house hackers looking to sell their property or get into bigger, more viable properties every two years, as they grow.

House hacking provides a unique opportunity for individuals to build wealth and take advantage of tax loopholes while simultaneously enjoying the benefits of homeownership. Through strategic real estate investment, one can reduce or eliminate housing expenses, build equity, benefit from long-term appreciation, and discreetly accumulate wealth. The added advantage of tax exemptions for staying in a residence for at least two years further enhances the financial benefits.

Note: As with any investment strategy, it is important to conduct thorough research, evaluate potential risks, and seek professional advice to make informed decisions when embarking on the house hacking journey.

INTEREST RATE BUYDOWNS

We often hear the term OPM when it comes to making money in real estate, but we rarely hear about paying for an interest rate buydown. An interest rate buydown is another financial strategy widely used by the stealth wealthy to lower the monthly mortgage payment on a home, if they even have a mortgage to begin with. It is typically used by homebuyers who are unable to qualify for a mortgage with the current interest rates. However, the wealthy have realized this to be a viable investment strategy. The strategy involves paying a lump sum of money at closing in exchange for a lower interest rate for the first few years of the loan. The lump sum of money is usually paid by the homebuyer, although it can also be paid by a third party, such as a government agency or a charitable organization. The interest rate buydown can make homeownership more affordable for those who would otherwise be unable to purchase a home, but it does require the homebuyer to have some cash upfront. It can also be done by lenders to offer more competitive interest rates in order to be more attractive to potential customers.

An example of an interest rate buydown would be as follows:

> A homebuyer is looking to purchase a home that costs $300,000 and is taking out a 30-year fixed-rate mortgage. The current interest rate is 4%, which would result in a monthly mortgage payment of around $1,432 (not including taxes and insurance).

> The homebuyer wants to buy down the interest rate to 3.5% for the first three years of the loan. To do this, the homebuyer pays a lump sum of $12,000 at closing. In exchange, the interest rate on the loan is reduced to 3.5% for the first 36 months of the loan. After 36 months, the interest rate will adjust to the current market rate. As a result, the homebuyer's monthly mortgage payment for the first 36 months would be around $1,335 (not including taxes and insurance), which is $97 less than it would have been with the original interest rate of 4%.

It's important to notice that even though the payments are smaller in the short term, the total interest paid is higher in the long term with this option, so this should be considered before making the decision.

NO DOWNPAYMENT LOANS - JUST GET IN!

The stealth wealthy understand the importance of simply 'getting into the game.' They know the many advantages one has when participating in this capitalistic society, whether it be tax or wealth-building advantages. And they even go to extreme lengths to participate if they aren't able to get in the traditional way. I can share those ways (which I will later in the chapters), but I'd rather give you a way to get into the game and play. So, allow me to introduce NACA loans or no downpayment loans.

NACA stands for Neighborhood Assistance Corporation of America, a non-profit organization that provides affordable homeownership solutions to individuals with low to moderate incomes. NACA offers no downpayment loans that allow first-time homebuyers to purchase a home without making a downpayment. To qualify for a NACA no downpayment loan, you must meet certain requirements, including having a steady income and a good credit score. You must also attend a homebuyer workshop and counseling session offered by NACA, where you will learn about the homebuying process, budgeting, and credit repair. To attend a NACA homebuying workshop, visit the NACA website and register for an upcoming event. The workshop will cover the homebuying process, including the benefits of NACA's no down-payment loan program. After completing the workshop, you will be required to attend a homebuyer counseling session. During the session, a NACA counselor will review your financial situation and help you develop a budget that works for you. They will also provide advice on credit repair and help you understand your mortgage options.

YOUR APPLICATION PROCESS

Once you have completed the workshop and counseling session, you can submit your application for a no downpayment loan through the NACA website. The application will require you to provide documentation of your income, expenses, and assets. After your application is submitted, you will be assigned a NACA mortgage counselor. Your counselor will work with you throughout the homebuying process, helping you find a home that fits your budget and negotiating with the seller on your behalf. Once you have found a home and your loan has been approved, you will close on your home. NACA's no downpayment loan program allows you to purchase a home without making a down-payment, saving you money upfront. This can help you build wealth over time by allowing you to invest your money elsewhere.

NACA MAXIMUM ACQUISITION COST

While you can purchase a property in a large geographic area, there are limits based on your Member Status (i.e., Priority or Non-Priority) and NACA's maximum acquisition cost. Your purchase price plus any repair escrow funds (i.e., funds for repairs to be completed after closing) cannot exceed your approved Maximum Mortgage Amount or NACA's current maximum loan amount limits. You cannot exceed the below limits by reducing the principal.

Area Type Single Two-Family Three-Family Four-Family

Most Areas: $484,350 - $931,600

High Cost: $726,525 - $1,397,400

Use the button below to open the spreadsheet to determine whether a property is in a standard, medium, or high-cost area.

NACA's no downpayment loan program is an excellent option for first-time homebuyers looking to purchase a home and build wealth. By attending a homebuying workshop and counseling session, you can learn about the homebuying process and qualify for a no downpay-ment loan. Working with a NACA mortgage counselor can help you find a home that fits your budget and negotiate on your behalf, making the homebuying process easier and more affordable.

So, In a world where everyone chases shiny, flashy investments for quick gains, the truly wealthy know the secret to success lies in the business of "boring". Boring strategy's and investments quietly grow and make consistent profits. The key is to focus on value, cash flow, predictability, and think long-term. By investing in companies with strong foundations, adaptability, and a competitive edge, you build a safety net of steady cash flow that provides stability during market uncertainties. Avoiding zombie companies that rely on debt and government handouts, and even exploring real estate through clever strategies like house hacking, and leveraging favorable programs to simply 'get in', can further enhance your wealth-building journey. Learn to embrace the "boring" path and join the ranks of the stealth wealthy, as it may lead you to true and consistent wealth, where one day you could be sipping a fancy drink on a tropical beach, all thanks to those seemingly unexciting investments.

> **"If something sounds too good
> to be true, nine times out of ten,
> your intuition is correct."**

CHAPTER 5: COVID-19: THE GREAT WEALTH TRAP

The COVID-19 pandemic had a significant impact on the global economy as governments implemented lockdowns and social distancing measures to slow the spread of the disease. Businesses were forced to close their doors, and many people lost their jobs. As a result, the credit market tightened, and many businesses and consumers found it difficult to borrow. The Federal Reserve (Fed) responded by implementing several measures to support the credit market and the economy.

One of the main actions taken by the Fed was to lower the federal funds rate to near zero. This made it cheaper for banks to borrow money, which, in turn, made it cheaper for businesses and consumers to borrow money. The Fed also launched several programs to provide liquidity to the financial system, such as the Main Street Lending Program, which provided loans to small and medium-sized businesses. Additionally, the Fed supported households and small businesses through the CARES Act, which provided financial assistance to those affected by the pandemic.

While the Fed's actions during the COVID-19 pandemic were crucial in stabilizing the credit market and supporting the economy, there were also downsides to these decisions. One downside was the potential for hyperinflation. With interest rates near zero, there was a risk that the increased money supply could lead to higher inflation. This could erode the purchasing power of consumers and make it more expensive for businesses to borrow money.

> *"When money flows freely, speculation takes the lead. But as the cost of money rise, value investing plants its seed."*
>
> **-UNKNOWN**

Another downside was the impact on savers. As interest rates were lowered, the returns on savings accounts and other fixed-income investments also decreased, which can be particularly hard for retirees and others who rely on interest income. This can make it more difficult for people to save for retirement or other long-term goals. Moreover, some critics argue that the Fed's actions may have widened the wealth gap between the rich and the poor. The Fed's programs to support the financial system mainly benefited large financial institutions and investors, while small businesses and low-income individuals may not have had the same access to the programs. This can exacerbate economic inequality and make it harder for people to climb the economic ladder. Furthermore, the Fed's actions may have also led to a stock market bubble. The low-interest rates and the Fed's quantitative easing program led to a flood of money into the stock market, causing stock prices to rise to unsustainable levels. This can lead to an economic downturn when the bubble bursts. Additionally, the low-interest rates and quantitative easing also led to a flood of money into the crypto market, causing crypto prices to rise to unsustainable levels. This can lead to an economic downturn when the bubble bursts.

While the Fed's actions during the COVID-19 pandemic were crucial in stabilizing the credit market and supporting the economy, they also had downsides such as the potential for inflation, increased government debt, decreased returns on savings, widening the wealth gap, and the crypto and stock market bubble. These downsides must be considered as the Fed navigates a complex and ever-changing global economy in the future. It's important to recognize that the Federal Reserve's actions have both positive and negative consequences, and it's essential to weigh the pros and cons when making decisions that affect the economy and the financial well-being of individuals and businesses.

TURNING CRISIS TO CASH: SEIZING OPPORTUNITIES IN ANY MARKET

Despite the downsides of the Federal Reserve's actions during the COVID-19 pandemic, there were still opportunities for individuals to make money in this market. Here are a few ways that people potentially profited in this current economic environment:

1. Investing in the stock market: With the Fed's quantitative easing program and low-interest rates, there had been a flood of money into the stock market. This caused stock prices to rise to unsustainable levels, but it also presented an opportunity for investors to make money by buying stocks at a lower price and selling them at a higher price. However, it was important to note that there was a risk of a stock market bubble and the potential for an economic downturn when the bubble burst.

2. Investing in bonds: As interest rates were near zero, bonds were considered a safer investment as they provided a fixed income and a low-risk return. The bond market was also considered to

be less volatile than the stock market, which was a good option for risk-averse investors.

3. Investing in real estate: With low-interest rates, it was cheaper to borrow money to invest in real estate. This presented an opportunity for investors to purchase properties at a lower price and potentially make a profit when the market recovered.

4. Investing in small businesses: With the Fed's Main Street Lending Program, small and medium-sized businesses had access to more funding. Investing in these businesses was a great way to support local communities and potentially make a profit.

It was important to note that investing in any market came with risk, and it was essential to do your own research and consult a financial advisor before making any investment decisions. Additionally, it was important to consider the downsides of the Federal Reserve's actions and the potential impact on the economy before making any investment decisions.

Let's explore some of the strategies that can help you achieve this goal, even in a higher-for-longer rate environment.

First, investing in high-quality stocks of companies with strong fundamentals can be a great way to achieve long-term growth. Look for companies with a solid financial position, a competitive advantage, and a track record of consistent growth. Additionally, diversifying your portfolio by investing in a variety of stocks from different sectors and industries can help to reduce risk. One popular strategy is to invest in index funds, which provide broad exposure to the stock market and can help diversify your portfolio.

Another strategy is to invest in real estate. Despite the potential for rising interest rates, real estate can still offer a good return on investment over the long term. Look for properties that have the potential for appreciation, such as properties in up-and-coming neighborhoods or properties that can be renovated or developed. Investing in rental properties can also provide a steady stream of passive income, which can help to grow your wealth over time.

Investing in start-up companies is another way to potentially achieve a high return on investment. Start-up companies that are in a high-growth industry, have a strong management team, and a solid business model have a greater potential to grow and deliver a large return on investment. This can be a riskier investment, but the potential rewards can be substantial.

Disclaimer:

It's important to note that investing in any market comes with risk, and it's essential to do your own research and consult a financial advisor before making any investment decisions. Additionally, it's important to consider the economic environment and the potential impact of interest rate changes on the assets you are considering investing in. Diversifying your investment portfolio and taking a long-term approach to investing can help to mitigate risk and increase the likelihood of achieving your goal of making a million dollars from a small investment.

Making a million dollars from a small investment is possible, but it requires a long-term approach and a well-diversified portfolio. By investing in high-quality stocks, real estate, and start-up companies, and by diversifying your portfolio, you can minimize risk and increase the chances of achieving your financial goals. Remember to do your own research and consult a financial advisor before making any investment decisions. With the right strategies and understanding of the market, you can work towards building wealth over time.

HABITS RARELY CHANGE: FEDERAL RESERVE

In the world of personal finance, it is important to understand the language used by central banks and financial institutions. Here lie two of the most commonly used terms. These words are meant to provide reassurance and stability, but they have been used to deceive the public time and time again.

Key Definitions to pay attention to:

1. Transitory - A Temporary Illusion

   The term "transitory" is used to describe a temporary change in economic conditions. This can include a temporary increase in inflation or a temporary decrease in unemployment. It is meant to reassure investors that any changes in the economy are not permanent and will not have long-term effects. However, as with the term "soft landing," the reality is often far from the promised reassurance.

2. Soft Landing - A Mirage of Stability

   A "soft landing" is a term used to describe a controlled slowdown of inflation and the economy, with the goal of avoiding a recession or economic downturn. It is meant to reassure investors and the public that the economy is stable and under control. However, the reality is that a soft landing is incredibly difficult to achieve, and more often than not, it is simply a mirage.

They say if you want to predict the future, follow history. In this case, if you want to make money this time around, follow the historical habits of the Fed. Throughout the history of the Federal Reserve, they've had a habit of overshooting both rate increases and decreases. So why on earth did anyone believe that the outcome of the 'transitory inflation' would work without a hard landing? This habit can be seen throughout the history of the Fed, starting with the 1970s when they raised interest rates too high, causing a recession in the early 1980s. The Fed then lowered interest rates too much, causing the savings and loan crisis of the late 1980s. In the late 1990s, the Fed raised interest rates too much, causing the dot-com bubble to burst. And more recently, the Fed lowered interest rates to zero during the 2008 financial crisis, leading to the current low-interest-rate environment.

> *"When too few goods chase too many dollars, that's called inflation."*
>
> **- JEREMIAH J. BROWN**

This habit of overshooting both rate increases and decreases can have major implications for investors and the overall economy. Through two monetary tools known as open market operations (setting interest rates for banks) and quantitative easing (printing new currency into existence, purchasing bonds, and other assets), the Fed has the ability to drastically influence the economy. When interest rates are raised too high, it can cause a recession and lead to a decline in the stock market and real estate values. When interest rates are lowered too much, it can lead to a bubble in the stock market and real estate prices. Therefore, understanding the historical habits of the Fed is important for making investment decisions and understanding the potential impact of their actions on the economy. While the Fed has promised that the current low-interest-rate environment is transitory, history suggests otherwise.

This chart points to the effects that a low-rate environment can lead to:

The Worst Years Ever For the U.S. Stock Market		
Year	S&P 500	Reason
1931	-43.8%	Great Depression
2008	-36.6%	Great Financial Crisis
1937	-35.3%	1937 Crash
1974	-25.9%	1973-74 Bear Market
1930	-25.1%	Great Depression
2002	-22.0%	Dot-Com Crash
1973	-14.3%	1973-74 Bear Market
1941	-12.8%	WWII
2001	-11.9%	Dot-Com Crash
1940	-10.7%	WWII
1957	-10.5%	1957-58 Recession

This list includes the only double-digit losses for the S&P in this time frame. It's happened 11 times.

FOLLOW THE FEDERAL RESERVE'S PIVOTS

When building stealth wealth, it is important to follow the Fed's pivots. Historical evidence shows that every time the Fed contracts the money supply, a panic, followed by a decline, and then a bank crisis, always follows. As rates increase and quantitative tightening continues, banks tend to tighten their lending standards and restrict their once 'loose' lending requirements. In other words, they cut back on lending out the money. This supply of money going down, as rates are going up, is a recipe for disaster in the markets. However, for those who have built up cash reserves, it can also breed an opportunity to take advantage of these downturns in the market. The way to protect yourself in a scenario like this would be to have a reserve account that includes short-term bonds, CDs, a money market account, and just outright cash. Having liquidity or the ability to easily convert assets into cash would allow you to quickly take advantage of purchasing undervalued assets or those that have experienced significant decline.

It's times like these where paying close attention to the Fed's pivots is more vital to your long-term portfolio than the assets themselves. So, if you believe that the Fed will continue to print fiat currency, you should have one strategy (to take advantage of low rates by buying up assets and increasing your cash flow). If you think our current Federal Reserve chair will take their hands off the switch and continue to raise interest rates for longer, your strategy should be to keep yourself liquid in that deflationary environment. It's important to be patient during periods of Fed tightening and hold onto a cash reserve and prepare for opportunities in the markets during these declines.

MARKET CYCLES: UNDERSTANDING THE PATTERN

Market cycles refer to the recurring pattern of growth and contraction in the stock market. These cycles can last anywhere from five to ten years, with the average cycle lasting approximately seven years. During a market cycle, investors have the opportunity to make significant profits by buying low and selling high. As you may know, the peak of the market cycle from 2009 to 2021 was pretty unusual.

Market cycles are characterized by four distinct phases:

1. Expansion

2. Peak

3. Contraction

4. Trough - During this period, there is a huge difference between asset prices and their true value. This period is where you can truly build real wealth.

5. (Repeat)

In the expansion phase, the economy is growing, and stock prices are generally rising. This phase is typically characterized by low unemployment, increased consumer spending, and rising corporate profits. As the expansion phase progresses, stock prices reach a peak, marking the beginning of the contraction phase. In the contraction phase, the economy slows down, and stock prices begin to fall. This phase is typically characterized by rising unemployment, decreased consumer spending, and falling corporate profits. As the contraction phase continues, stock prices reach a trough, marking the beginning of the next expansion phase. It's important to note that market cycles are not always predictable and can be influenced by a variety of factors, including political events, economic conditions, and natural disasters. However, understanding the pattern of market cycles can help you make informed investment decisions and maximize your profits.

> *"In an economy heavily dependent on cheap money, speculation is the winning strategy. When the tides shift and money becomes expensive, value investing becomes the winning strategy."*
>
> -JEREMIAH J. BROWN

THE FEDERAL RESERVE AND ITS IMPACT ON MARKET CYCLES

The Federal Reserve is the central bank that the United States is partnered with and is responsible for controlling the money supply and interest rates. These decisions can significantly impact the economy and stock market, influencing market cycles and shaping investment opportunities. For instance, when the Federal Reserve raises interest rates, it can lead to a decrease in consumer spending as people are less likely to borrow money for large purchases. This decrease in consumer spending can cause a decline in stock prices, as companies may experience lower profits and reduced growth. On the other hand, when the Federal Reserve lowers interest rates, it can stimulate consumer spending, leading to increased stock prices.

One of the most notable examples of the Federal Reserve's impact on the stock market was during the late 1990s. The Federal Reserve kept interest rates low, resulting in an unprecedented boom in the stock market known as the dot-com bubble. This period saw a surge in technology stocks and a frenzy of investment activity. While the bubble eventually burst, many astute investors were able to generate substantial profits by investing in tech stocks and capitalizing on the low interest rates.

The ultra-wealthy can profit from the Federal Reserve's mistakes by carefully analyzing the market and anticipating the impact of their decisions. They also have access to abundant resources and expertise that enable them to make informed decisions and minimize risk.

HOW TO PROFIT FROM MARKET CYCLES AND THE FEDERAL RESERVE

To join the ranks of the ultra-wealthy and profit from market cycles and the Federal Reserve, it's essential to educate yourself, stay informed, and make informed decisions. Here are some tips to help you get started:

1. Stay informed: Read financial news and stay up to date on the latest developments in the stock market and the economy. This will help you anticipate market fluctuations and make informed investment decisions.

2. Diversify your portfolio: Spread your investments across different industries and asset classes to reduce risk and maximize returns.

3. Utilize professional resources: Consider working with a financial advisor who can provide expert guidance and help you navigate the complex world of investing. A financial advisor can also assist you in developing a customized investment strategy that aligns with your financial goals and risk tolerance.

4. Avoid chasing returns: Instead of investing in stocks solely based on their recent performance, focus on well-established companies with a strong track record of growth and stability.

5. Be patient: Investing in the stock market requires patience, as market cycles can take time to play out. Avoid panicking and selling during a market downturn, as these periods often present the best opportunities for buying low and selling high.

6. Monitor the Federal Reserve: Pay attention to the Federal Reserve's decisions and how they impact the economy and stock market. This will help you anticipate shifts in the market and take advantage of investment opportunities.

Market cycles and the Federal Reserve's influence can provide significant opportunities for informed and strategic investors. By staying informed, diversifying your portfolio, utilizing professional resources, avoiding impulsive investments, being patient, and monitoring the Federal Reserve, you can profit from market cycles and the decisions made by the Federal Reserve.

THE IMPORTANCE OF THE CREDIT MARKET AND THE FEDERAL RESERVE'S ROLE IN MANAGING IT

In reality, the Federal Reserve doesn't prioritize the stock market; its focus is on the credit market. The credit market is a vital component of the economy that plays a crucial role in facilitating economic growth. It allows businesses and consumers to access credit, such as loans and financing, to invest in projects, purchase goods and services, and engage in economic transactions that drive growth. When the credit market functions well, credit is readily available to businesses and consumers at reasonable rates, promoting economic growth. This can be observed in vibrant downtown areas where new construction projects are underway, and small business owners are expanding their operations. Consumers can also purchase homes and cars and secure loans for education and other needs. All of this economic activity thrives due to the availability of credit and supports overall economic growth.

However, when the credit market tightens, businesses and consumers may struggle to borrow, which slows down economic growth. This can be seen in struggling communities with boarded-up storefronts and stagnant construction sites. Consumers may find it challenging to obtain loans for homes and cars, and small business owners may face difficulties in keeping their businesses afloat. All of this economic activity slows down, and the economy may enter a recession.

The Federal Reserve (Fed) plays a crucial role in ensuring the proper functioning of the credit market. They employ various tools and policies to promote a stable and healthy credit market. One of the primary tools used by the Fed is the federal funds rate, which is simply the interest rate at which banks can borrow money from each other overnight. By adjusting this rate, the Fed can influence the cost of borrowing for businesses and consumers. If the Fed believes that the economy is overheating, they may raise the interest rate to slow down borrowing and spending. Conversely, if the Fed believes that the economy is in a recession, they may lower the interest rate to make borrowing cheaper and encourage spending and investment. For example, during the 2008 financial crisis, the Fed lowered the federal funds rate to near zero to stimulate borrowing, spending, and help the economy recover. This policy helped improve the credit market and support economic growth. However, the Fed's role in managing the credit market is just one piece of the puzzle. The Fed must also navigate a complex and ever-changing global economy where events such as natural disasters, political turmoil, and technological advancements can have a profound impact on the credit market and the overall health of the economy.

IS THE FEDERAL RESERVE RESPONSIBLE FOR BRICS?

The United States of America was once the undisputed superpower of the world, with the largest and most powerful economy. Thanks to the Bretton Woods agreement established in 1944, the US dollar became the dominant currency for international trade. However, in 2020, something unprecedented happened in American history—the Federal Reserve printed 80% of all money ever printed in one year. This staggering amount of money signaled a dire economic situation for the country and served as a clear indication that the US dollar was losing its value, sending a warning to all investors. As the US dollar continues to depreciate, more countries are turning away from it and seeking alternative currencies for international trade. China, in particular, has been steadily reducing its reliance on the US dollar in recent years. It actively promotes the use of its currency, the yuan, in international trade, demonstrating the country's growing economic power. Recent years have witnessed rapid changes, and the rise of BRICS countries is a clear indication that the US is now facing tough competition in the global arena.

The rise of BRICS countries, including Brazil, Russia, India, China, and South Africa, is another clear indication that the US is facing stiff competition in the global arena. These countries are rapidly growing in power and challenging the dominance of the USA in international affairs. They are also promoting the use of their currencies in international trade, further challenging the dominance of the US dollar. These developments serve as a dire warning to investors. The world is changing rapidly, and traditional investment approaches may no longer be sufficient. Assets such as stocks, bonds, and real estate, which were once considered reliable, may no longer provide the necessary returns to secure financial futures.

NAVIGATION THE SHIFT

In order to navigate these uncertain times successfully, investors should consider a range of investment opportunities, including cash-flowing real estate, companies with strong balance sheets and a substantiated economic moat, as well as other alternative assets like land. It is important to have global exposure in these investments to capture diverse opportunities and mitigate risks. To enhance their investment portfolios, investors should also be open to alternative assets such as cryptocurrency, commodities, and precious metals. These assets provide diversification and serve as a hedge against inflation and currency devaluation.Moreover, investors should prioritize increasing their financial literacy and establishing a comprehensive financial plan that engages with Federal Reserve policy. This plan should involve setting clear goals, creating a budget, and devising a savings and investment strategy that aligns with their risk tolerance, financial objectives, and policy changes.

The rise of BRICS countries and the ongoing shift away from the US dollar indicate that the US faces strong competition in the global arena. As a result, caution and adaptability are essential for investors seeking success in these uncertain times. By remaining open to new opportunities and embracing alternative assets, investors can position themselves to thrive amidst changing market dynamics.

The past pandemic brought significant challenges to the entire global economy, but it also presented opportunities for individuals to seize. While the actions taken by the Federal Reserve during this time had downsides, such as the potential for inflation, deflation, and widening the wealth gap, an emergence of a potentially new global superpower, there were still avenues for people to make money. Investing in the stock market, bonds, real estate, and small businesses emerged as potential avenues for profit. However, the retracement of the free money that once flowed during the pandemic, presents a true example of why it is crucial to conduct thorough research, seek professional advice, and consider the potential risks associated with these invest-ments. By being mindful of the Federal Reserve's actions and the broader economic landscape, individuals can navigate these uncertain times and seize opportunities for financial success.

"**Gold is money, everything else is credit**"

-J.P. MORGAN

CHAPTER 6:

Alternative Investments - The New 60/40

In times of economic uncertainty, the wealthy often turn to alternative assets that have proven to be impervious to recession. These assets act as a safety net, protecting their wealth and providing stability during market volatility. Alternative investments are financial assets that do not fall into the traditional categories of stocks, bonds, and cash. Examples of alternative investments include real estate, private equity, commodities, and collectibles. The profitability of alternative investments can vary widely and is often dependent on the specific investment and market conditions. Some alternative investments may be more profitable than others, depending on an individual's risk tolerance and investment goals.

Hedge funds and private equity funds have historically been among the most profitable alternative investments. They are typically available only to accredited investors and tend to be less regulated than other types of investments. Real estate investments can also be profitable, particularly in a strong real estate market. Commodities can be profitable when prices are rising, but they can also be risky due to potential large price swings. Collectibles such as art and rare coins can also be profitable, but these investments can be illiquid and difficult to value.

Note: It's important to recognize that alternative investments come with a higher level of risk, and the potential for high returns often comes with a high level of risk. It is crucial to do your own research before making any investment decisions and consult with professional advisors.

While some of these assets, such as gold and silver, are well-known, others like cryptocurrencies, art, and collectibles are favored by the stealth wealthy. These assets act as a safety net, protecting their wealth and providing stability during market volatility. The evidence and stories support the claim that these assets are recession-proof and should be considered by investors looking to preserve their wealth during uncertain times.

AN ASSET VS. A STORE OF VALUE

I want to take a moment to debunk the notion of what truly constitutes an asset. From luxury cars to exotic pets, cryptocurrencies, high-end watches, and fine art, it seems like everything is considered an asset today. While all stores of value are assets, not all assets are stores of value. For example, a stock may be an asset, but it is not necessarily a good store of value because its value can be highly volatile and subject to rapid changes in market conditions. The same applies to high-end real estate. On the other hand, gold has been used as a store of value for thousands of years because it is a tangible asset that is relatively stable and has a long history of retaining its value over time.

Properties, particularly in desirable locations, have the potential to appreciate over time and provide a stable store of value. For example, a property that was purchased for $100 million free and clear could offer a great way to preserve your wealth and ride the wave of inflation. However, it requires substantial holding costs associated with taxes, maintenance, insurance, and upkeep that can eat into its value over time. Similarly, cryptocurrencies like Bitcoin have gained popularity as assets, but their volatile nature and lack of intrinsic value make them a risky store of value. While they have the potential for significant returns, they are also prone to sharp declines in value, making them unsuitable for those seeking a stable long-term store of value. When it comes to luxury items such as high-end watches, fine art, or exotic pets, their value is often subjective and dependent on individual tastes and trends. While they can appreciate in value, their value is highly susceptible to fluctuations in the market and changing consumer preferences. Therefore, while they may be considered assets, they may not necessarily serve as reliable stores of value.

Ultimately, the distinction between an asset and a store of value lies in the stability and reliability of their value over time. An asset is a broader term that encompasses various items with value, while a store of value refers specifically to an asset that retains its value or appreciates over time, serving as a reliable means of preserving wealth. It is crucial to thoroughly evaluate the characteristics and market dynamics of different assets before considering them as potential stores of value within one's investment strategy.

THE FUTURE OF BANKING AND CRYPTO

Silicon Valley, home to some of the world's wealthiest and most innovative individuals, hides a startling truth: more than 85% of the deposits held by the region's banks are uninsured. This revelation carries significant implications for the future of banking and the investments of the affluent. Uninsured bank deposits, in this context, refer to deposits lacking the backing of the Federal Deposit Insurance Corporation

(FDIC), which safeguards depositors in the event of bank failures. In simpler terms, if a bank fails and holds uninsured deposits, those depositors may struggle to recover their funds.

"The Future of Banking: More than 85% of Silicon Valley's Bank Deposits are Uninsured."

THE RESURGENCE OF BITCOIN

The high percentage of uninsured bank deposits in Silicon Valley reflects a growing trend among the discreetly wealthy: an increasing skepticism towards traditional banking institutions and a quest for alternative ways to preserve wealth. This is where Bitcoin, Ethereum, and central bank digital currencies (CBDCs) enter the picture. These digital assets operate in a decentralized manner, free from governmental or financial institution control. Moreover, they boast robust security, utilizing advanced cryptography to guard against fraud and hacking.

Bitcoin and Ethereum, in particular, have gained popularity as stores of value and investment assets for the future. Over the past decade, both cryptocurrencies have experienced significant value growth. Bitcoin, for instance, reached an all-time high of nearly $65,000 in April 2021 before stabilizing at around $20,000. Ethereum, often referred to as digital silver, is not merely a digital currency but also a platform that enables developers to create decentralized applications and smart contracts. Ethereum's primary objective is to provide a foundation for developers to construct and deploy various blockchain-based applications, including decentralized finance (DeFi), non-fungible tokens (NFTs), and more. Due to their unique attributes, both Bitcoin and Ethereum have emerged as ultimate safe-haven digital assets for long-term investments. Operating as ultimate digital scarcity networks, they remain unaffected by inflation or government manipulation, making them a hedge against economic uncertainty. Unlike other crypto-currencies prone to price volatility, under-collateralized exchanges, or dog coins, Bitcoin stands as a stable investment option that has withstood the test of time. Its market capitalization has consistently grown, and despite price fluctuations, it has shown impressive overall value appreciation.

> *"One must differentiate between speculating on a cryptocurrency's use-case versus understanding its actual economics."*
>
> **- JEREMIAH J. BROWN**

OWNING BITCOIN AS AN ALTERNATIVE INVESTMENT STRATEGY

Bitcoin transcends being merely a digital asset; it represents a revolutionary technology capable of reshaping our perspective on money and finance. While exchanges like Allemida Research, FTX, SVB, and others may come and go, Bitcoin itself is here to stay, much like gold. Its use case as a safe-haven asset, impervious to inflation and government manipulation, positions it as an excellent long-term investment. Despite price fluctuations, Bitcoin continues to gain popularity and acceptance worldwide. By investing in Bitcoin for the long haul, individuals have the potential to benefit from its appreciation and safeguard their wealth against inflation and economic instability. Therefore, if you seek a safe-haven digital asset for investment, Bitcoin should undoubtedly top your list. The future of finance is currently being shaped, and with Bitcoin, you can actively participate in it.

CASH FLOW FOR CRYPTO?

Welcome to the exciting world of staking crypto, where your crypto investments can generate a consistent cash flow. Imagine earning interest on your digital assets while waiting for their value to appreciate, all through the process of staking. Whether you're an experienced investor or embarking on your crypto journey, cryptocurrency staking opens up a realm of opportunities to make your money work harder for you. In this captivating realm, cryptocurrencies such as Ethereum and Bitcoin go beyond being digital currencies; they transform into vehicles for financial growth. Let's explore the fascinating concept of staking crypto, where cash flow intersects with decentralized finance, offering boundless possibilities.

Let's delve into and unveil the potential of this opportunity.

When you stake crypto, you invest your money in certain cryptocurrencies like Ethereum or Bitcoin and receive rewards in return. It's akin to lending your money to the crypto network and earning interest on the staked amount. Staking differs from speculation or relying on the crypto's price to rise. Through staking, you earn regular income, akin to receiving a monthly allowance or rental income from owning a property. It's a way to make your money work for you and generate cash flow.

To ensure you don't lose your money while staking, follow this strategy. First, choose cryptocurrencies with robust and reliable networks, such as Ethereum or Bitcoin, which enjoy trust and established status in the crypto world. Next, find a secure blockchain infrastructure that allows you to stake your crypto. Research and select a reputable platform with a solid track record and positive reviews. When you're ready to stake, decide how much crypto you want to invest. It's wise to start with an amount you're comfortable with, avoiding risking too much. Stake a portion of your crypto holdings and securely store the rest in a reliable wallet.

Remember, staking entails risks. Like any investment, crypto prices can be volatile, rising and falling rapidly. Therefore, conduct thorough research and monitor the market. Nonetheless, by choosing dependable cryptocurrencies and using trusted staking platforms, you can mitigate risks and increase the likelihood of earning a stable income. Overall, staking crypto is a means of investing your money and generating regular interest without relying solely on price appreciation. It's a smart cash flow strategy that aids in long-term savings growth. Just remember to select appropriate cryptocurrencies and platforms while remaining aware of the associated risks.

GLOBAL ADOPTION

Central bank digital currencies (CBDCs) are digital versions of a country's fiat currency. While still in development, some countries like China have already begun testing CBDCs. CBDCs offer similar benefits to cryptocurrencies, including decentralization and security, but they are backed by a government or central bank. The rise of these digital assets reflects a shift in how we perceive money and wealth. The future of banking might not rely on traditional institutions but instead focus on decentralized and secure digital assets. However, it's essential to note that investing in these assets carries risks, and investors should conduct thorough due diligence and understand the potential risks involved. While cryptocurrencies and CBDCs offer numerous advantages, they are also subject to volatility and regulatory uncertainties.

The fact that over 85% of Silicon Valley's bank deposits are uninsured should serve as a wake-up call for the wealthy and a signal of the growing trend towards alternative methods of storing and investing wealth. Bitcoin, Ethereum, and CBDCs offer a new path forward, but investors should approach with caution and educate themselves about the potential risks and rewards associated with these assets.

THE ART OF INVESTING

The art world has experienced significant transformation in recent years due to technological advancements and industry globalization. As the art market continues to expand, more people are recognizing art as an asset class. However, fully capitalizing on art's potential as an asset class necessitates the establishment of a credit market. Let's explore the concept of the art credit market, its significance, and how it is revolutionizing the way we view and trade art.

The art credit market refers to the financial system that provides funding for purchasing artworks, either by borrowing against existing works or using them as collateral for loans. In recent years, there has been a notable increase in the utilization of lines of credit against artwork. This trend arises from the growing recognition of art as a valuable asset class. The steady increase in art's value over the past few decades is one of the primary reasons for the surge in lines of credit against artwork. According to a report by Artprice, the global art market reached a record high of $64 billion in 2018, and it is expected to continue growing in the future.

THE RISE OF LINES OF CREDIT AGAINST ARTWORK

Institutional investors, such as Yieldstreet, an online investing platform, are driving the market even further. They recently added an $11 million junior loan participation to its Diversified Art Fund 1, which pools together art loans backed by well-known artists such as Andy Warhol and Roy Lichtenstein. The fund, driven by analytics from the company's Athena Art Finance unit, has sold nearly $40 million in loans to investors, targeting a net return of 9.5%. Another example is Sotheby's, one of the world's largest auction houses, which is also looking to expand into this market. Although the company is still in the early stages of its expansion, industry experts expect that Sotheby's could launch its own fund or securitization structure, packaging art loans as an investment opportunity for clients or outside investors. As more financial institutions enter this market, we can expect to see more investment opportunities for art owners and investors in the future.

This market has emerged in response to the increasing demand for art as an investment, allowing individuals and institutions to finance their purchases, which would otherwise be difficult to achieve. The art credit market provides liquidity to the art market by enabling investors to purchase works of art without tying up large amounts of capital. The significance of the art credit market lies in its ability to view art as a true asset class. An asset class is defined as a group of investments that have similar characteristics and are subject to the same market forces. The existence of a credit market is crucial for establishing art as an asset class, as it allows for the creation of investment products and the trading of art as a financial instrument.

The art credit market is changing the way we view and trade art in several ways. It institutionalizes and increases the accessibility of art as an investment, allowing for free market participation, and provides liquidity to the market overall. The art credit market has made it easier to sell art and helps to stabilize prices.

WINE & DINE 'TIME'

Fine wines and luxury watches can be considered alternative investments as they do not fall into the traditional categories of stocks, bonds, and cash. Wine, as an investment, has been gaining popularity in recent years due to the rare and unique nature of fine wines, which makes them appealing to collectors. The value of a bottle of wine can increase due to the rarity of the vintage, the reputation of the winery, and the quality of the wine. Here's how:

Rarity:

Wine is perishable, and as the stocks decrease, the remaining bottles become more valuable. Some wines are produced in limited quantities and highly sought after by collectors. For example, a bottle of Château Margaux from a highly rated vintage such as 1945 or 1961 can fetch a price in the tens of thousands of dollars.

Reputation:

The reputation of the winery is also important. Wineries that have a long history of producing high-quality wines are more likely to see their wines appreciate in value. For example, a bottle of Dom Perignon from a prestigious vintage such as 1962 or 1990 can fetch a price in the thousands of dollars.

Quality:

The quality of the wine is also a crucial factor in determining its value. Wines that are highly rated by wine critics and experts are more likely to appreciate in value. Wines that have received high scores from organizations such as Wine Spectator, Wine Advocate, and Decanter are considered to be of high quality and can fetch a higher price.

It's worth noting that the wine market is relatively illiquid, and the value of a bottle of wine can fluctuate depending on factors such as storage conditions, wine authenticity, and market conditions. Therefore, conducting thorough research, consulting with professionals, and maintaining a long-term perspective are important. Additionally, the wine market is not highly regulated, which could be a concern for some investors.

A MILLION THROUGH CUSTOMS - HIGH-END WATCHES USED TO HIDE WEALTH

The surveillance of money has always presented a problem for those looking to fly under the radar. To these individuals, referred to as the stealth wealthy, money can be viewed as a system of control. Whether through everyday transactions, travel, investing, saving, or digitization, there is a sense of accounting and surveillance of money transportation. Don't believe it? Try carrying a bunch of gold bars worth over $50K through an airport. Not only would they not allow it past the detectors, but they would also confiscate it on the assumption that you're a criminal trying to expand into other territories, even without a court order. The same rules apply if you try to carry $100k in cash.

However, with a Rolex Batgirl or a Tiffany Patek 57-11 valued at well over $2 million around your wrist, you'll be able to walk through the airport with over $2 million in your possession and comfortably reach your destination without anyone confiscating it. In a way, this is a legal way to transport large amounts of money across borders without evidence of carrying significant sums.

Besides the more "nefarious" reasons mentioned, investing in luxury watches can also be a great way to diversify your portfolio and potentially earn a high return on your investment for several reasons:

1. Limited supply and high demand: Many luxury watches are produced in limited quantities, leading to high demand and increased value over time.

2. Brand reputation: Luxury watch brands such as Rolex, Patek Philippe, and Omega have established reputations for quality and craftsmanship. These brands hold their value well over time and can appreciate.

3. Collector appeal: Luxury watches can be considered collectibles, and certain models are highly sought after by collectors, driving up their value.

4. Store of value: Similar to gold or real estate, watches have been used as a store of value to protect against inflation, currency fluctuations, and economic uncertainty.

5. Hedge against market volatility: Luxury watches, as an alternative investment class, can be less correlated to other asset classes such as stocks and bonds. They can help diversify an investment portfolio, reducing overall risk and volatility.

6. Limited production: Some luxury watches are very rare and produced in limited quantities.

It's important to note that investing in luxury watches can be considered high risk, and thorough research, consultation with professionals, and portfolio diversification are crucial. It's also important to be selective and knowledgeable about the specific watch you are considering for investment. Like wine, the watch market is relatively illiquid, and prices can fluctuate based on factors such as brand reputation, model rarity, and market conditions.

Side note: As with any alternative investment, thorough market research and consulting with professionals are important steps before making any decisions. These are relatively high-risk investments.

ELOC - STOCK PORTFO-LIO AS AN ALTERNATIVE

While discussing alternative assets, it's important to note the term "alternative." This chapter is about alternative investment strategies, and one effective strategy is tapping into the equity of your stock portfolio, known as a "stock line of credit." A stock line of credit is a type of loan that allows individuals or businesses to borrow money using their stock portfolio as collateral. With a stock line of credit, borrowers can borrow up to a certain percentage of their stock portfolio's value and use the funds for investment or other expenses. They repay the loan with interest while retaining the ability to hold and trade the stocks during the loan period.

Stock lines of credit can be useful for investors looking to seize market opportunities when they lack immediate cash. They can also assist businesses in covering short-term expenses like payroll or inventory costs. One of the main benefits of this loan type is the lower interest rate compared to unsecured loans, as the stocks serve as collateral. However, it's crucial to acknowledge the inherent risk associated with stock lines of credit, as the value of the collateral (stocks) can fluctuate. If the stock value drops below a certain level, additional collateral may be required, or the stocks may need to be sold, resulting in potential losses. Before taking out a stock line of credit, it's important to consider your financial goals, investment strategy, ability to repay the loan, and seek professional advice.

BORROW AGAINST YOUR BONDS

If you haven't realized yet, there are multiple ways to tap into your assets without selling them, and the same holds true for bonds. It may be possible to borrow against your bonds, but it depends on the type of bond and the bond agreement terms. Certain bond issuers, such as government entities and large corporations, may offer bondholders the option to pledge their bonds as collateral for a loan, known as a bond pledge loan. The loan terms, including interest rate and repayment conditions, will vary based on the bond issuer and the lender.

Another way to borrow against your bond is by using it as collateral for a margin loan. Brokerage firms provide margin loans to clients who wish to borrow money for investing in stocks, options, or other securities. In this case, the bond acts as collateral, and the borrower pays interest on the borrowed amount.

Caution: It's important to note that, like any loan, there is a risk that the value of the collateral (bonds) may decrease, and the borrower may be unable to meet margin calls, potentially leading to the liquidation of the bonds. Consider the bond's terms and the issuer's creditworthiness before using bonds as collateral. It's also crucial to remember that borrowing against your bond means potentially losing control over it and leaving it at the mercy of the lender. Consulting with a financial advisor before making any decisions is a wise choice.

THE SECRET INVESTMENT - A.I.

It's no secret that the wealthy are always looking for new ways to grow and protect their wealth. One of the most recent and promising areas of investment that the wealthy are quietly exploring is artificial intelligence (A.I.). One of the key reasons why the wealthy are turning to A.I. as an investment opportunity is that it offers a level of precision and efficiency that is unmatched by human labor. A.I. algorithms can process and analyze vast amounts of data in a fraction of the time it would take a human being, and they can do it with a level of accuracy that is simply not possible with human analysis. This increased precision and efficiency can lead to higher profits for companies that are able to effectively utilize A.I. technologies. As the wealthy are always seeking new opportunities to increase their wealth, it makes sense that they would be interested in investing in A.I.

AI USED TO SCALE EFFICIENCY

According to a 2017 study, every single job in our world will be taken over by artificial intelligence. A.I. is already being used in a wide range of industries, from healthcare to finance to transportation. And as the technology continues to advance, the potential for A.I. to revolutionize these industries and create new opportunities for growth and profitability is enormous. Let's examine the companies that are currently at the forefront of A.I. technology, such as Alphabet Inc. (GOOGL), which has heavily invested in A.I. through its Google subsidiary. We will also take a closer look at companies in industries such as healthcare, finance, and transportation, where A.I. is already being used to improve efficiency and accuracy. Another reason why the wealthy are turning to A.I. as an investment opportunity is that it offers a level of security and predictability that is hard to come by in other areas of the stock market. A.I. algorithms can analyze vast amounts of data and make predictions about future market trends with a high degree of accuracy. We will take a closer look at companies such as NVIDIA Corporation (NVDA), which is using A.I. to create powerful new tools for data analytics and machine learning, and IBM (IBM), which has made significant investments in A.I. research and development. As we delve into the world of A.I. investment, it's important to remember that the field is still relatively new and A.I. technology is continually evolving. That's why it's essential to do your due diligence and research the companies and technologies involved before making any investments.

Another reason why the wealthy are turning to A.I. as an investment opportunity is that it offers a level of security and predictability that is hard to come by in other areas of the stock market. A.I. algorithms can analyze vast amounts of data and make predictions about future market trends with a high degree of accuracy. This means that companies that are able to effectively utilize A.I. technologies are more likely to be able to predict and prepare for market fluctuations, which can lead to higher profits and less risk for investors. So, if you're one of the stealth wealthy and looking for new opportunities to grow and protect your wealth, A.I. may be worth considering as a potential area of investment. Just be aware that the field is still relatively new, and A.I. technology is continually evolving, so it's important to do your due diligence and research the companies and technologies involved before making any investments.

The stealth wealthy are turning to A.I. as a new area of investment because it offers a level of precision, efficiency, predictability, and security that is unmatched by human labor. With the potential to revolutionize industries and create new opportunities for growth and profitability, A.I. is an exciting and promising area of investment for the wealthy. As we have seen, AI has emerged as a key driver of innovation and growth across a wide range of industries, from healthcare to finance to transportation. The potential for AI to revolutionize these industries and create new opportunities for growth and profitability is enormous. And with 90% of all companies predicted to incorporate AI within the next 20 years, it's clear that this technology will play a major role in shaping the future of our world.

WHAT DOES THIS MEAN FOR INVESTORS?

So, how can you take advantage of this emerging trend to build wealth and secure your financial future? Well, one way to invest in AI is by focusing on companies that are at the forefront of AI research and development. These companies are investing heavily in AI technology and are well-positioned to benefit from its widespread adoption across various industries. Microsoft (MSFT), an active investor in the new A.I. phenomenon, ChatGPT, Alphabet Inc. (GOOGL), NVIDIA Corporation (NVDA), and IBM (IBM) are just a few examples of companies that are leading the way in AI development. However, investing in individual companies can be risky, as their fortunes can rise and fall depending on a variety of factors, including market conditions, regulatory changes, and competition.

AI ETFS

Another way to invest in AI is through ETFs that focus on the technology sector. These ETFs provide exposure to a diversified portfolio of companies that are involved in developing and using AI, reducing the risk associated with investing in individual companies. One example of an AI-focused ETF is the Global X Robotics & Artificial Intelligence ETF (BOTZ). This ETF invests in companies that are involved in the production, development, or use of robotics and AI technologies. It provides exposure to a broad range of companies, including those involved in industrial automation, healthcare robotics, and autonomous vehicles. Another AI-focused ETF is the AI Powered Equity ETF (AIEQ), which uses an AI-powered algorithm to select stocks based on their potential for future growth.

Investing in AI through ETFs can be an effective way to capitalize on this emerging trend while minimizing risk. However, it's important to do your due diligence and research the ETFs you are considering before making any investments. Look for ETFs with a strong track record of performance and a portfolio of companies that are well-positioned to benefit from the growth of AI. In conclusion, AI has emerged as a key driver of innovation and growth across various industries, and its potential to change the way we live and work cannot be ignored. Investing in AI can be a powerful way to build wealth and secure your financial future. Whether you choose to invest in individual companies or through AI-focused ETFs, the key is to do your research and invest wisely to reap the benefits of this exciting and promising new technology.

NOTE: As always, it's important to do your due diligence and research the companies and technologies involved before making any investments.

LAND - THE SIMPLE ALTERNATIVE ASSET

Stealthy wealthy investors are always on the lookout for ways to diversify their portfolios and hedge against market fluctuations. While traditional investments like stocks and bonds are popular choices, there are also many alternative investments to consider. One such option is land, particularly farmland, which has a negative correlation to the stock market and can even appreciate in tough economic times. The saying goes, "Land is one of the only assets that God isn't making any more of," and the laws of supply and demand are more prevalent than ever in this asset class.

Although farmland may be an economically viable investment, what if I told you that investing in solar farming is an even more unique and sustainable option? Solar farming involves buying land and leasing it out to a solar farm company, which will then use the land to generate solar energy. This investment strategy provides a steady stream of passive income, often for many years, making it a smart way to diversify your portfolio and hedge against market fluctuations. Additionally, investing in solar farming has a positive impact on the environment by reducing dependence on fossil fuels and contributing to a more sustainable future.

HOW DO I LEASE MY LAND OUT TO A SOLAR FARM?

The first step in this investment strategy is to find a location that is ideal for solar farming. Solar farm companies prefer flat land with good access to the power grid and receives ample sunlight throughout the year. They also prefer larger plots of land, typically over 50 acres, to build solar farms. However, you can still consider community-scale or smaller-scale solar facilities if you own at least 5 acres of land.

HOW DOES IT WORK?

Once you've found the right location, it's time to lease the land to a solar farm company through a lease agreement that outlines the terms and conditions. The rental amount will depend on factors such as the land's size, sunlight exposure, and prevailing market rates for solar farm leases in the area. Lease rates can range from $500 to $2,000 per acre per year. The lease term can span from 20 to 40 years, depending on the agreement between the landowner and the solar farm company. Investing in solar farming has many advantages. It provides a steady stream of passive income for many years and is a sustainable investment with a positive impact on the environment. Moreover, it allows you to diversify your portfolio and hedge against market fluctuations.

There are various solar farm companies to choose from when leasing your land, such as Cypress Creek Renewables. They offer long-term lease agreements with competitive rates and work with landowners to ensure compliance with local land use laws.Investing in solar farming by buying land and leasing it out to a solar farm company is a smart and sustainable investment strategy. With the increasing demand for alternative energy sources and the clear benefits of solar farming, it's an investment that can pay off for years to come. So, why not consider investing in solar farming to diversify your portfolio while contributing to a better future for our planet?

HOW TO BEGIN THE PROCESS OF OWNING AND LEASING OUT LAND

Now that you understand the basics of buying land and leasing it out to a solar farm company, here's a step-by-step guide to help you get started:

Step 1: Research
Start by researching the solar energy potential in your area. This will help you determine if your land is suitable for solar farming. You can find this information online or by contacting a solar energy consultant in your area.

Step 2: Find the Right Location
Check with local land agents to see if there's any available land in your area suitable for solar farming. You can also conduct your own online research or directly contact solar energy companies to explore leasing opportunities.

Step 3: Contact Solar Farm Companies
Reach out to potential solar farm companies in your area and express your interest in leasing your land for solar farming. You can find these companies online

or through local solar energy consultants. Provide them with information about your land, including location, size, and any other relevant details. This will help them determine if your land meets their requirements.

Step 4: Negotiate Lease Terms
When a solar farm company expresses interest in leasing your land, start negotiating the lease terms. This includes discussing the rental amount, lease duration, and any other conditions important to you or the solar farm company. Take your time to review the lease agreement carefully before signing. It may be wise to consult with a lawyer or financial advisor to ensure your full understanding of the terms.

Step 5: Sign the Lease Agreement
Once you've negotiated the lease terms and are satisfied with the agreement, sign the lease agreement. Congratulations, you are now officially a solar landowner!

Note: Landowners interested in leasing their land for solar farming should consider factors such as location, solar resource, transmission access, interconnection, and land use regulations. Solar companies seek locations with high sunlight levels throughout the year and proximity to transmission lines or substations for connecting the solar farm's energy to the power grid. Some solar companies also consider local zoning laws and regulations when selecting land for lease to ensure compliance with local land use laws.

GOLD - THE ALTERNATIVE HONEST INVESTMENT

Gold has long been used by the stealthy wealthy as an alternative investment, and there are several reasons for its enduring popularity. In the past, when gold and silver served as the primary forms of money, their units were not interchangeable like our modern-day currencies. They came in odd sizes, different weights, and purities, making it challenging to assign an exact price to goods and services. This created a certain level of uncertainty and made determining the true value of something a guessing game.

One crucial aspect of gold and silver is their limited quantity. Unlike fiat currencies such as the Dollar, Pound, or Yuan, which can be printed or manipulated by governments and central banks, gold and silver cannot be easily expanded. Their scarcity prevents arbitrary inflation, maintaining their value over time. The same ounce of pure gold holds the same store of value in Egypt as it does in the United States, India, Russia, or China. This universality makes gold a reliable medium of exchange across borders.Another significant attribute of gold is its durability. Gold has proven its resilience throughout history, as the same gold that was used by the Egyptians 5,000 years ago, can still be melted and reused today. Its enduring nature has allowed gold to withstand the test of time and maintain its value over millennia. While the physical properties of gold limit its portability, the development of smaller divisible units and the underlying support of digital money have made it as portable as traditional currencies.

THE INFLATION HEDGE

Gold and silver are often referred to as an "honest" investment strategy because they have consistently preserved and proved their value throughout history. For a form of money to be considered honest, it must maintain its purchasing power over extended periods. In contrast, the purchasing power of fiat currencies like the Dollar has significantly eroded over time. Since the establishment of the Federal Reserve in 1913, the Dollar has lost over 97% of its purchasing power. This loss of value is evident when comparing the price of gold and real estate to the declining Dollar. Gold and real estate tend to increase in value as the currency depreciates. This inverse correlation stems from the fact that assets like gold and real estate act as a hedge against inflation, absorbing the expanding currency supply. The reliability of gold and silver as honest money becomes more apparent when considering the historical failures of fiat currencies. Throughout time, numerous rulers and nations have experienced the collapse of their fiat currencies, many of which were not backed by precious metals. The inherent flaw in debt-backed currencies is their reliance on confidence. Once confidence in the ability to repay mounting debts wavers, the currency's value can quickly plummet. This has led to a 100% failure rate for debt-backed fiat currencies throughout history.

Gold's status as the ultimate form of money has endured for thousands of years. Its limited quantity, universality, durability, and ability to preserve value over time make it highly sought after by the stealthy wealthy. While it is classified as a commodity rather than a currency, gold's global use and dominance contribute to its role as a store of wealth and protection against inflation. As an alternative investment, gold continues to offer stability and security in an ever-changing financial landscape.

Alternative Investments and assets form a unique investment category. With the rise of information accessibility, many traditional assets have already been explored and exploited. These alternative assets encompass a wide range of non-traditional investment options, including private equity, hedge funds, real estate investment trusts (REITs), commodities, cryptocurrency, collectibles, and more. What sets them apart is their potential to generate uncorrelated returns compared to traditional asset classes like stocks and bonds. This can help mitigate risk and enhance overall portfolio performance. These assets remain open to those willing to embark on a journey of discovery, making them an enticing prospect for savvy and stealthy investors who seek to stay ahead of the curve and capitalize on emerging opportunities.

"Taxes are essentially the unavoidable price of participating in society."

-JEREMIAH J. BROWN

CHAPTER 7:

Beyond the IRS: Legally Reducing Your Tax Burden

When it comes to personal finance, everyone wants to keep as much of their hard-earned money as possible. But did you know that some individuals, known as the "stealth wealthy," can legally avoid paying taxes? It may sound too good to be true, but with careful planning and execution, anyone can become part of this exclusive group. Each country and jurisdiction has its own tax codes, and in the United States, the federal tax code comprises over 70,000 pages of rules and regulations. Additionally, state and local governments have their own tax codes, showcasing the numerous incentives available to owners and investors.

However, it is crucial to understand the distinction between tax avoidance and tax evasion. Tax avoidance involves using legal methods to minimize tax liability, while tax evasion entails breaking the law to avoid paying taxes. This discussion revolves around tax avoidance, not evasion, which is perfectly legal and even encouraged through tax deductions and credits.

OPPORTUNITY OR 'TAX ELIMINATION' ZONES

As you explore the realm of personal finance, you may encounter intimidating terms and concepts. One such concept is capital gains, which refers to profits made when selling an asset for more than its purchase price. While capital gains can enhance wealth, they can also result in substantial tax bills. Fortunately, there is a way to defer those taxes by investing in income-producing Opportunity Zone properties.

Opportunity Zones are designated areas in the United States that require economic development. The government offers tax incentives to investors who invest in these areas, and one of the benefits is the ability to defer capital gains taxes.

HERE'S HOW IT WORKS:

Suppose you sell a stock, business, or real estate asset, generating a $100,000 profit. Normally, you would owe capital gains taxes on that profit. However, if you invest the $100,000 in an Opportunity Zone property, you can defer paying those taxes until 2026 or until you sell the Opportunity Zone property, whichever comes first. This means you have more money available for investment and wealth growth, rather than paying taxes on your gains. Moreover, if you hold the Opportunity Zone property for at least 10 years, you may be eligible for a permanent exclusion of capital gains taxes on the property's appreciation. Essentially, any profit made on the property after 10 years would be tax-free.

Disclaimer: Investing in Opportunity Zone properties may not suit everyone, so it is vital to conduct thorough research and understand the associated risks. However, for those looking to defer capital gains taxes and invest in disadvantaged areas, it can be a win-win situation. Not only can you defer and potentially avoid taxes, but you can also contribute positively to communities in need, all while growing your wealth. Like the other tax-saving strategies we will discuss, investing in Opportunity Zones can significantly benefit your long-term financial goals. If you seek a way to defer capital gains taxes and invest in economically disadvantaged areas, consider investing in Opportunity Zone properties. By doing so, you will have more funds available for investment, potentially avoiding taxes on gains altogether, and simultaneously making a positive impact on communities.

THE CHARITY TAX LOOPHOLE

Charitable Remainder trusts are intriguing tools that offer both philanthropic benefits and tax savings for individuals. While they are commonly utilized by the stealth wealthy, including those desiring privacy, they are also accessible to average individuals seeking tax breaks while supporting charitable causes. A charitable remainder trust is a legal arrangement where an individual (the donor) transfers assets, such as cash, securities, or real estate, to a trust. The trust then pays an annual income to the donor or another beneficiary for a specified period, which could be for life. After the trust term concludes, the remaining assets in the trust are distributed to charitable organizations designated by the donor.

Advantages:

1. One primary benefit of a charitable remainder trust is the immediate tax deduction the donor receives for the charitable portion of the gift. When the assets are transferred to the trust, the donor can deduct the present value of the future charitable contribution from their income taxes. This deduction reduces the overall tax liability and can result in significant tax savings.

2. Another advantage of a charitable remainder trust is the potential for capital gains tax savings. When the trust sells appreciated assets, such as stocks or real estate, it can do so without incurring an immediate capital gains tax liability. This allows the donor to avoid paying taxes on the appreciation and potentially reinvest the full amount into income-generating assets within the trust. Consequently, the donor can generate income from the trust while deferring the capital gains tax.

Additionally, charitable remainder trusts offer flexibility in terms of income distribution. The donor or beneficiaries can receive a fixed income for life, a specific period, or even a fluctuating income based on the trust's annual valuation. This flexibility can be particularly advantageous for retirees or individuals seeking supplemental income during specific periods, such as funding college tuition.

While charitable remainder trusts provide tax advantages and support charitable causes, it is important to note that they have certain requirements and limitations. For instance, the donor must transfer assets irrevocably to the trust, meaning they cannot reclaim them once transferred.

The donor must ensure that the charitable remainder is at least 10% of the initial fair market value of the assets contributed to the trust. In other words, when establishing the trust, the donor must ensure that at least 10% of the total value of the assets they transfer into the trust will ultimately go to the charitable organizations upon the termination of the trust. To take advantage of this tax break, average individuals can explore the possibility of setting up a charitable remainder trust by consulting with an estate planning attorneys experienced in charitable planning. These professionals can provide guidance on setting up the trust, ensuring compliance with tax laws, and selecting charitable organizations aligned with the donor's philanthropic goals.

Note: It's worth noting that tax laws and regulations may vary between countries and regions, so it is essential to consult with professionals well-versed in the relevant tax code. The charitable remainder trusts offer a unique opportunity for individuals to support charitable causes while potentially reducing their tax liability. Although they are frequently utilized by the wealthy, they can also be accessible to average individuals seeking tax advantages. By understanding the benefits and requirements of charitable remainder trusts, individuals can make informed decisions regarding their financial and philanthropic goals.

WORK PLAN FOR TAX SAVINGS

Another option for the stealth wealthy is to utilize a Health Savings Account (HSA). An HSA is a tax-advantaged savings account used to pay for medical expenses. Contributions to an HSA are tax-deductible, and any earnings from the account are tax-free. Additionally, withdrawals made to cover qualified medical expenses are also tax-free.

The stealth wealthy often take advantage of tax-deferred retirement accounts, such as traditional IRAs and 401(k)s. These accounts allow you to contribute pre-tax income, meaning you won't pay taxes on that income until you withdraw it in retirement. This enables you to reduce your taxable income currently while saving for the future. The "stealth wealthy" legally avoid paying taxes through various strategies, including tax-exempt municipal bonds, charitable giving, health savings accounts, and tax-deferred retirement accounts. By carefully planning and executing these strategies, you can minimize your tax liability and retain more of your hard-earned money. Tax avoidance is entirely legal and encouraged by the government, so there's no reason not to seize these opportunities to save. In this chapter, we will delve deep into how the wealthy employ tax advantages to build wealth and increase their financial well-being.

THE MORE YOU KEEP

Most people believe that the only way to accumulate wealth is by increasing their income. While a higher income can undoubtedly help, it is not the sole determinant of financial success. In fact, some of the world's wealthiest individuals have discovered that the secret to building wealth lies not in earning more money, but in keeping more of the money they already have. One of the most effective ways to achieve this is by utilizing tax strategies to minimize your tax liability.

The IRS tax code is complex and ever-changing, but there are legitimate ways to legally reduce your taxes and retain more of your money. This is where cost segregation comes into play. Cost segregation is a tax strategy employed by real estate investors to accelerate depreciation on their investment properties, thereby reducing their tax burden. The idea behind cost segregation is that different components of a property, such as the roof, HVAC system, and flooring, have different depreciation schedules. By segregating these components and depreciating them separately, investors can claim a larger tax deduction in the earlier years of ownership when it is most valuable.

For example, let's say you own a commercial property that cost $1 million. Without cost segregation, you would typically depreciate the entire property over 39 years, resulting in a depreciation expense of $25,641 per year. However, with cost segregation, you might be able to depreciate certain components of the property over 5, 7, or 15 years, allowing for a depreciation expense of $100,000 or more in the first year alone. This means you could potentially save tens of thousands of dollars in taxes in the initial years of ownership.

MAKE MONEY THROUGH DEPRECIATION

Cost segregation study is just one of many tax strategies that can help you legally reduce your tax liability and keep more of your hard-earned money. Other strategies include maximizing deductions, taking advantage of tax credits, and utilizing retirement accounts like IRAs and 401(k)s. By working with a qualified tax professional who understands the intricacies of the tax code, you can develop a personalized tax strategy that works for you. According to a study by the National Bureau of Economic Research, the top 1% of taxpayers in the US pay an effective tax rate of just 18.8%, compared to the 27.1% paid by the middle class. This is because the wealthy have access to a range of tax strategies and loopholes that allow them to legally reduce their tax liability. By utilizing these same strategies, you too can keep more of your money and build wealth over time.

Building wealth is not just about making more money. It's about utilizing smart financial strategies that allow you to keep more of the money you already have. Tax strategies like cost segregation can be incredibly effective in reducing your tax liability and putting more money back in your pocket. By working with a qualified tax professional and staying up-to-date on changes to the tax code, you can develop a personalized tax strategy that works for you and helps you achieve your financial goals.

TURN LOSSES INTO WINS - TAX LOSS HARVESTING

The wealthy understand that every financial loss can be an opportunity to minimize their tax burden. Through a strategy called tax loss harvesting, they turn their losses into wins and reduce their overall tax liability. In this chapter, we will explore the benefits of tax loss harvesting and offer a step-by-step guide to approaching this hack.

WHAT IS TAX LOSS HARVESTING?

Tax loss harvesting is a strategy that involves selling securities or assets that have lost value to offset the capital gains tax liability on other investments. By doing this, investors can lower their tax bill and potentially earn a higher after-tax return. For example, suppose you have a portfolio with $100,000 in gains and $50,000 in losses. By selling the securities with losses, you can offset the gains and reduce the capital gains tax you owe.

2023 ASSET DOWNTURN - AN EXAMPLE

2022 and 2023 were challenging years for investors with the recent downturn in the stock market. However, this presents a unique opportunity for tax loss harvesting. Suppose you invested $10,000 in stock ABC, and the value has dropped to $5,000. By selling the stock, you can realize a $5,000 loss that can be used to offset capital gains on other investments. Suppose you have $5,000 in capital gains from other investments. By using the loss to offset the gains, you can reduce your tax liability to $0.

STEP-BY-STEP GUIDE TO TAX LOSS HARVESTING

1. Review Your Portfolio: Begin by reviewing your portfolio for securities or assets that have lost value.

2. Identify Losses: Identify any securities or assets that have lost value and can be sold to realize a loss.

3. Assess Your Capital Gains: Calculate your capital gains for the year. If your losses exceed your gains, you can use the remaining losses to offset up to $3,000 of ordinary income.

4. Avoid the Wash-Sale Rule: To avoid triggering the wash-sale rule, do not repurchase the same security or asset within 30 days of selling it.

5. Repeat the Process: Tax loss harvesting is an ongoing process that can be repeated each year to minimize your tax liability.

Tax loss harvesting is an effective strategy that the wealthy use to minimize their tax liability. By turning losses into wins, investors can potentially earn a higher after-tax return. With the recent asset downturn in 2022, there is no better time to implement this strategy. Follow the step-by-step guide, and with careful planning and execution, you too can make the most of your financial losses. Remember, to move like the wealthy, you must understand this one principle: every loss is an opportunity to minimize your tax burden and increase your wealth.

STEALTH WEALTH AND THE ART OF INSURANCE

Building wealth is an art that has been perfected by many successful individuals and families throughout history. One of the best examples of this is the Rockefeller family, who used a combination of smart investments and insurance policies to grow their wealth and secure their financial future. Let's explore the concept of stealth wealth and how the Rockefellers used insurance to leverage their wealth-building efforts.

The Rockefellers were masters of the concept of stealth wealth, using it to build their family dynasty and maintain their hierarchy as a global elite. They did so while avoiding the negative connotations that often come with being wealthy. One of the ways that the Rockefellers used their wealth to their advantage was through the use of trusts and insurance. They recognized that insurance policies could not only protect their wealth but also help them leverage it for their benefit. For example, the Rockefellers were among the first individuals to purchase life insurance policies in bulk, using the policies to secure loans and fund their business ventures. By using their insurance policies as collateral, the Rockefellers were able to access the funds they needed to invest in their businesses, real estate, and grow their wealth.

The Rockefellers also used insurance policies to reduce their tax burden. How? By using life insurance policies to transfer wealth from one generation to the next, they were able to minimize their estate taxes and pass their wealth on to their children and future generations in a tax-efficient manner. This allowed them to keep more of their wealth and continue growing it over time. The Rockefellers were masterful in their use of insurance to leverage their wealth-building efforts. By combining stealth wealth and the art of insurance, they were able to secure their financial future for generations. By following their example, you can use insurance to protect and grow your wealth, while avoiding the negative connotations that often come with being wealthy. Remember, insurance policies are not just for protecting your wealth; they can also be used as a tool to build and leverage it.

The Rockefellers used insurance in several ways to leverage their wealth-building efforts:

1. Using life insurance policies as collateral: The Rockefellers were among the first individuals to purchase life insurance policies in bulk and use them as collateral to secure loans. By doing so,

they were able to access the funds they needed to invest in their businesses and grow their wealth.

2. Minimizing tax burden: The Rockefellers used life insurance policies to transfer wealth from one generation to the next, thereby minimizing their estate taxes (through the death benefit tax exemption), and allowing them to keep more of their wealth.

3. Diversifying their investment portfolio: The Rockefellers invested in a diverse portfolio of assets, including stocks, bonds, and insurance policies. By doing so, they were able to spread their risk and ensure that their wealth was protected in case of a market downturn.

4. Preparing for unexpected events: The Rockefellers purchased insurance policies to protect their wealth and prepare for unexpected events, such as the death of a family member or a natural disaster. By doing so, they were able to secure their financial future and ensure that their wealth would be protected in case of an emergency.

BUILDING YOUR FAMILY BANK:

The Rockefellers used insurance policies in a strategic manner to protect, leverage, and grow their wealth. By combining stealth wealth with the art of insurance, they were able to secure their financial future and make a positive impact on the world. Here is a step-by-step approach to being your own version of a Rockefeller family:

First: Open up the trust and appoint yourself as the trustee, so you maintain complete control of the trust.

Second: Have the trust purchase a cash value life insurance policy. This policy is at your discretion,

> but try to ensure the policy has a cash value that you
> are able to borrow from.
>
> Lastly: You can borrow from the policy to invest in
> other assets and use the cash flow from the assets to
> pay down the loan and generate a profit thereafter.

Make sure that the family trust is the beneficiary of the life insurance so that when someone passes away, the trust can be fully replenished.

THE MONTANA CAR PURCHASE TAX HACK: WHAT THE WEALTHY DON'T WANT YOU TO KNOW

As you stroll through the streets of Beverly Hills or the Upper East Side, you'll undoubtedly see an array of luxurious vehicles, from Lamborghinis to Bentleys. But have you ever wondered why some of these cars have Montana license plates, despite their owners living in California or New York? It's all part of a little-known loophole that the wealthy have been exploiting for years: the Montana car purchase tax hack.

This tax hack involves buying a car in Montana, a state with no sales tax on vehicles, and then registering the car in another state with a much higher sales tax, such as California or New York. This results in significant savings on the purchase price of the vehicle, as well as the avoidance of any potential luxury taxes that some states impose. The Montana car purchase tax hack has been a closely guarded secret of the wealthy for years, and it's not hard to see why. By using this loophole, a buyer can save tens of thousands of dollars on the purchase of a luxury vehicle.

For example:

A $100,000 car purchased in Montana would save the buyer around $9,000 in sales tax compared to purchasing that same car in California.

Despite the incredible savings, the wealthy are keeping this hack a secret. The reason for this is simple: if everyone knew about it, the loophole would be closed, and the savings would disappear. As it stands, this loophole is legal, and there is no indication that any state or federal government is moving to close it.

So how do you take advantage of the Montana car purchase tax hack?

First, you'll need to find a dealership in Montana that's willing to sell you the car. This may involve some negotiation, as some dealerships are aware of the loophole and may not want to risk losing their Montana sales tax exemption. Once you've purchased the car, you'll need to register it in your home state, which will involve paying the sales tax on the purchase price. However, even with the sales tax, you'll still come out ahead, thanks to the significant savings from purchasing the car in Montana.

While the Montana car purchase tax hack is legal, it's worth noting that some states are cracking down on it. For example, California is investigating individuals who have registered luxury cars in Montana but have failed to pay California use tax on the vehicles. This use tax is designed to capture tax revenue from out-of-state purchases, and California is cracking down on those who try to evade it.

The Montana car purchase tax hack is a closely guarded secret of the wealthy, and for good reason. By taking advantage of this loophole, a buyer can save tens of thousands of dollars on the purchase of a luxury vehicle. While it may be legal, it's not without risks, and it's likely that some states will start cracking down on those who use this loophole to avoid paying their fair share of taxes. Nevertheless, it remains a powerful tool in the arsenal of those who can afford to take advantage of it.

THE ACCOUNTANTS' G-WAGON

In recent years, the purchase of luxury vehicles, particularly the G Wagon, has seen a significant rise in popularity. From celebrities to successful entrepreneurs, the G Wagon has become a symbol of status and success. But why has this specific vehicle garnered so much attention, and how have tax incentives influenced this trend?

The Mercedes-Benz G Wagon, also known as the G Class, was initially designed for military use but has since evolved into a luxury SUV favored by the elite. The vehicle's rugged exterior, coupled with its high-end interior and advanced technology, has made it a popular choice for those who seek both functionality and luxury. The G Wagon's exclusivity and limited availability have added to its appeal. In some cases, the waitlist for a G Wagon can be up to a year, which only adds to its desirability. However, it's not just the allure of the G Wagon that has driven its rise in popularity. Tax incentives have played a significant role in making the vehicle more accessible to buyers. One tax incentive that has influenced the purchase of luxury vehicles like the G Wagon is Section 179 of the Internal Revenue Code. This section allows businesses to deduct the full purchase price of qualifying equipment and/or software purchased or financed during the tax year. This deduction can be up to $1,050,000 for the 2022 tax year, which can significantly reduce a company's tax liability.

To add, the Tax Cuts and Jobs Act of 2017 has expanded the definition of qualifying property under Section 179 to include certain improvements to nonresidential real property, such as roofs, HVAC systems, and security systems. This means that a business that purchases a

G Wagon for business use could potentially qualify for the Section 179 deduction.

The question remains, does Section 179 work for lease vehicles as well? The answer is yes.

The Tax Cuts and Jobs Act of 2017 has expanded the definition of qualifying property under Section 179 to include certain leasehold improvements. This means that a business that leases a G Wagon for business use could potentially qualify for the Section 179 deduction.

However, it's essential to note that the tax deduction is only available for vehicles that are used for business purposes. If the vehicle is used for personal use, the tax deduction would not apply.

While the Section 179 tax deduction has been a significant factor in the rise of luxury vehicle purchases like the G Wagon, it's worth noting that this incentive of 100% bonus depreciation is set to expire at the end of 2022, going down to 80% in 2023, and 60% in 2024. The future of this tax deduction is unclear, but it's very likely that Congress will either extend it or make modifications to the policy. As the saying goes, 'the rules are written by those who own the gold.'"

WARNING: BEWARE OF THE POTENTIAL DRAWBACKS OF 179/BONUS DEPRECIATION!

While it may seem like a great way to save on taxes in the short term, taking full depreciation on an asset can lead to a depreciation recapture tax on its sale. This means that you could end up owing taxes on a gain even if you sell the asset for less than its original purchase price. So, before taking advantage of this tax deduction, make sure you fully understand the potential risks and consult with a tax professional. Failure to do so could result in a costly mistake that you may regret later. For example, let's say you bought a g wagon for $100,000, and the next year you decide to sell it for $90,000, which would represent a $10,000 loss. You may think it's a 10k loss, but in fact, it would be considered a $90,000 gain, and you will be subject to paying the tax on this 'gain'. When you depreciate the car down to zero dollars, your cost basis became zero. To avoid making a costly mistake, seek professional advice and thoroughly understand the risks associated with this tax deduction. Don't let the lure of short-term savings blind you to the long-term consequences.

THE AUGUSTA RULE

As the sun sets over the sprawling greens of Augusta National Golf Club, a mysterious and intriguing story of tax deductions unfolds. The Augusta Rule, embedded in the tax code, has been a well-kept secret among the elite for years. But now, it's time for everyone to know the truth about this rule and how it can save you money on your taxes.

It all began with the U.S Open Championship, which took place in a rural yet fascinating location known as Augusta, Georgia. As the wealthy golf enthusiasts flocked to this idyllic location, they discovered a loophole in the tax code that allowed them to claim deductions by renting their houses for 14 days or less. Yes, you read that right. If you own a house and rent it to your own business for a fair and justified amount, you can claim that amount as a deduction on your tax return. This rule was created by the IRS, and it's all thanks to the popularity of the Augusta golf tournament.

Now, you may be thinking, "This sounds too good to be true. What's the catch?" The truth is, there isn't one. As long as you follow the guide-lines set forth by the IRS, you can take advantage of this tax deduction and save yourself some serious money.

HOW THE AUGUSTA RULE WORKS:

But how exactly does this work? Let's break it down. Say you own a house and your business needs a space to hold a meeting or event. You can rent out your house to your business for up to 14 days at a fair price, and you don't have to claim the income on your personal tax returns. Yet, your business can claim that rental expense that it "paid you" as a deduction on your tax return. Not only does this benefit you financially, but it also allows you to use your own space for your business needs, saving you the trouble of renting out a separate venue. Plus, you get to keep your home private and secure, without the hassle of strangers coming in and out. Of course, as with any tax deduction, there are some guidelines you must follow. You can only rent out your house for 14 days or less per year, and the rental income must be 'reasonable' and 'justified', whatever that means. But as long as you adhere to these rules, you can take advantage of the Augusta Rule and save yourself some serious cash come tax season.

The Augusta Rule may seem mysterious and awe-inspiring, but it's actually a practical and beneficial tax deduction that may of the stealth wealthy use, and it can save you money and provide a convenient space for your business needs. So, next time you find yourself in Augusta, Georgia, remember the Augusta Rule and the benefits it can provide. Because the stealth wealthy do!

THE STEALTH INVESTORS HEDGE INFLATION WITH THE I - BONDS STRATEGY

The popularity of investing in I Bonds has risen in the past three years, and this can be partly attributed to concerns about inflation. Stealth investors may turn to I Bonds as a way to protect against inflation because the inflation rate component of I Bonds is adjusted semi-annually based on changes in the Consumer Price Index (CPI). This means that the interest rate on I Bonds will adjust upward in response to increases in inflation, which can help investors maintain the purchasing power of their money.

The rise in the popularity of I Bonds over the past three years may also be due to the fact that the fixed interest rate component of I Bonds has been relatively attractive compared to other types of fixed income investments. For example, in the current low-interest-rate environment, the fixed rate on I Bonds has been relatively high compared to other types of savings accounts, CDs, or Treasury bonds.

Another factor that may have contributed to the rise in popularity of I Bonds is that they are backed by the U.S. government and are considered a low-risk investment. This makes them attractive to investors seeking a safe haven for their money during periods of economic uncertainty.

When bond yields increase, the value of existing bonds decreases, all else being equal. This is because the coupon payments on the existing bonds become relatively less attractive to investors compared to newly issued bonds that have higher coupon rates to reflect the higher market interest rates. To understand why this happens, it's important to understand the relationship between bond prices and yields. When a bond is issued, it has a fixed coupon rate that determines the regular payments that the bondholder will receive. However, as market interest rates change, the yield on the bond may become more or less attractive to investors.

THE 'CONS' OF I-BOND SPECULATION:

If market interest rates rise, then new bonds issued in the market will generally have higher coupon rates to reflect the higher yields that investors demand. This means that the coupon payments on the new bonds will be relatively more attractive to investors than the coupon payments on existing bonds with lower coupon rates. As a result, the price of existing bonds will fall to make them more competitive with the new bonds. Conversely, if market interest rates fall, then new bonds issued in the market will generally have lower coupon rates to reflect the lower yields that investors demand. This means that the coupon payments on existing bonds with higher coupon rates will be relatively more attractive to investors than the coupon payments on new bonds with lower coupon rates. As a result, the price of existing bonds will rise to make them more competitive with the new bonds.

It's also worth noting that the supply of new bonds in the market does not directly affect the value of existing bonds. However, if the supply of new bonds is significantly greater than the demand for bonds, then the increased supply could put downward pressure on bond prices in general, including the prices of existing bonds.

When buying I Bonds, it's important to understand how changes in bond yields can affect the value of the bonds. I Bonds are inflation-protected savings bonds issued by the U.S. Treasury. The interest rate on I Bonds consists of a fixed rate and an inflation rate. The fixed rate is set when the bond is issued and remains the same for the life of the bond, while the inflation rate is adjusted semi-annually based on changes in the Consumer Price Index (CPI). If market interest rates rise, the fixed rate on newly issued I Bonds may be higher to reflect the higher yields that investors demand. However, existing I Bonds will still have the same fixed rate as when they were issued, which may make them relatively less attractive to investors compared to new I Bonds with higher fixed rates. This can lead to a decrease in the value of existing I Bonds, all else being equal.

Conversely, if market interest rates fall, the fixed rate on newly issued I Bonds may be lower, which can make existing I Bonds relatively more attractive to investors. This can lead to an increase in the value of existing I Bonds, all else being equal. It's worth noting that changes in bond yields and interest rates are just one factor that can affect the value of I Bonds. The inflation rate, which is adjusted semi-annually based on changes in the CPI, can also affect the value of I Bonds. Additionally, other economic and financial factors such as defaults, opportunity cost, or hidden fees when purchasing a bond can also impact the value of I Bonds and other investments.

Reminder: It's important to recognize that tax avoidance is a legitimate practice sanctioned by governments worldwide. It allows individuals to take advantage of the incentives and benefits provided by the tax code to optimize their financial situations. By understanding and navigating these complex tax laws, anyone can explore opportunities for maximizing their savings and retaining more of their hard-earned income. Nevertheless, it's crucial to approach tax planning and avoidance with integrity and within the boundaries of the law. Engaging in illegal activities, such as tax evasion, not only carries severe consequences but also undermines the principles of fairness and accountability upon which our tax systems are built. The focus should always be on utilizing legal strategies, such as proper tax planning, asset structuring, and taking advantage of tax-advantaged vehicles, to minimize tax liabilities.

"To turn \$100 into \$110 is time
and work. To turn 100 million into
\$110 million is inevitable."

-UNKNOWN

CHAPTER 8:

The True Cost of Time

Time, the enigmatic sibling of our existence, is a powerful force that binds us all. It often mocks us, tauntingly eluding our grasp as we chase after its fleeting essence. The concept of time, in its very essence, represents stealth and mystery. And what is the currency that we choose to sacrifice at the altar of time? If you said money, you're absolutely correct. Money often seduces the masses with promises of wealth and prosperity, believing that it holds the key to happiness and success. However, money, like time, is a construct. It reminds us of this sort of phantom-like entity that weaves its treacherous web around your desire to be fulfilled. But what if I told you that the stealth wealthy place their highest value on their time rather than their money? Would you believe me?

Let me provide you with an example:

Rich = Money: $1 million dollars, I'm rich!

Wealth = Time: $1 million dollars!? How many days
can I go without working, or how many days can

my family go without working, while supporting the current lifestyle that I have?

This is difficult to comprehend, but the only way to truly pursue wealth is to essentially stop chasing the 'bag', and instead start chasing your time. You must reverse engineer the traditional mindset of chasing the bag to build real wealth; otherwise, you'll be chasing the tail of acquiring and consuming.

> *"You want to take 6 years of my time? It will cost you X millions of dollars."*

When it comes to investing, the stealth wealthy have a unique understanding of the value of their time. They approach their investments with a strategic mindset, knowing that time is a critical factor in building long-term wealth. This mindset allows them to sacrifice short-term gains for the sake of long-term success. One of the keys to their success is the understanding that investments require time to grow and mature. This means that they are willing to invest in assets that may not yield immediate returns. Instead, they look for investments that have the potential to grow steadily over time, producing significant returns in the long run while generating some form of cash flow in the interim. This mindset requires patience and discipline, as they must be willing to hold onto their investments for extended periods, even during times of market volatility. Moreover, the wealthy carefully weigh the potential risks and rewards of each investment opportunity, taking into account the opportunity cost of their time. This means that they are very selective about the opportunities they pursue and the amount of time they dedicate to each investment. They estimate the potential cost of spending time on a project versus the potential earnings from that project. By doing so, they are able to make informed decisions about which opportunities are worth pursuing and which are not.

Remember: The true definition of wealth is time. For example, the founder of Amazon earns about $2,400 a second. It would take about two weeks for the average employee of that same company to earn that same $2,400.

TIME VS. MONEY

For example, let's consider a scenario where a wealthy investor is presented with a new business opportunity that offers significant potential for a high return on investment. However, the entrepreneur requires a substantial amount of the investor's time to help launch the business. The wealthy investor recognizes the value of their time and takes into account the opportunity cost of dedicating six years to this project. They estimate that committing to this project for six years would cost them $10 million in potential earnings. Another example could be choosing to purchase an appreciating asset as an investment rather than a vehicle, which could potentially be a liability and incur costs. This decision is made with the aim of leveraging the bonus depreciation to recapture taxable income. With these considerations in mind, the wealthy individual can carefully evaluate the opportunity and determine if the potential rewards outweigh the cost of their time.

The stealth wealthy also understand the significance of diversification in their investment strategy. They distribute their investments across various asset classes and industries, minimizing risk and maximizing long-term returns. This strategy requires patience and discipline, as it may take years or even decades for some investments to yield substantial results. However, the payoff can be substantial, as a well-diversified portfolio can provide a steady stream of income and capital appreciation over time.

Additionally, the wealthy recognize that investing is an ongoing process and not a one-time event. They consistently evaluate their investments, make necessary adjustments, and remain committed to their long-term goals. They understand that building wealth is a marathon, not a sprint, and are willing to invest the time and effort required to achieve their objectives. They possess a unique understanding of the value of time when it comes to investing. They approach their investments strategically, sacrificing short-term gains for long-term success. They carefully assess the potential risks and rewards of each investment opportunity, taking into account the opportunity cost of their time. This enables them to make informed decisions about which opportunities are worth pursuing. Through diversification and continuous evaluation, the wealthy can build lasting wealth, demonstrating that investing is indeed a marathon, not a sprint.

UNMADE MONEY, THE SILENT LOSS

The wealthy view money not earned as money lost, recognizing the fundamentally different nature of the game they play. It is important to understand that money is not merely a means of exchange; it is a game with rules to follow and strategies to master. The wealthy embrace this understanding and approach money with a different mindset than the average person. They perceive every opportunity as a potential source of income and are constantly seeking new ways to generate wealth. They understand that money is not a finite resource but can be created and multiplied through intelligent investments and calculated risks. It's not solely about the money, but also about the mindset. The wealthy have an abundance mindset, believing that there is always more to be attained. They view money as a tool for achieving their goals and are unafraid to take risks to realize them. They refuse to settle for mediocrity, always striving for more.

> *"The pain of discipline is less*
> *than the pain of regret."*

This mindset is not exclusive to the wealthy; it can be learned and adopted by anyone. It starts with changing your perspective on money and seeing it as a tool to achieve your goals, rather than an end in itself. It's about understanding that money is not a finite resource, but one that can be created and multiplied through smart investments and calculated risks. By understanding the wealth mindset and adopting the strategies of the wealthy, you too can join the ranks of the financially successful. Remember, money not made is money lost, and the wealthy understand this.

Now it's your turn to join the game and start winning.

A PROFIT IS A PROFIT

It's never easy to let go of something that has been a part of you for so long, but taking a step back and re-evaluating your priorities can lead to a brighter future. In the world of personal finance and building wealth stealthily, this often means knowing when to take a profit and not dwelling on missed opportunities.

When we invest our time, money, and emotions into something, we often have a specific price or outcome in mind. However, things don't always go as planned. You might receive an offer that is lower than your expectations, or the market might take a downturn, causing your investment to lose value. In such situations, it's easy to feel like you've lost something, but it's important to remember that a profit is still a profit. Dwelling on what could have been will only hold you back. When it comes to personal finance, it's crucial to align your investments with your goals. If your sole purpose is to make a profit, remember that there are always risks involved. However, if you invest with a long-term perspective and a solid understanding of your risk tolerance, you'll be better equipped to handle the ups and downs of the market.

Similarly, it's important to know when to cut your losses and move on. It's easy to get attached to something that isn't working out, whether it's because of the time or money you've invested in it. However, continuing to pour resources into a losing venture will only lead to further losses. Take a step back, objectively assess the situation, and consider whether it's worth continuing to invest in something that isn't working. Sometimes it's better to take a smaller profit or even a loss and move on to something with better potential for success. Remember, the value of taking a profit or cutting your losses isn't just about the money. It's about freeing yourself from the emotional burden of a failed investment and allowing yourself to focus on the opportunities that lie ahead. By being mindful of your goals, risk tolerance, and ability to let go, you can create a personal finance strategy that empowers you to move forward and achieve your dreams.

CAPITALIZING ON BOOM AND BUST CYCLES OF LIFE: UNLEASHING THE POWER WITHIN

In the realm of personal finance, navigating the ever-changing tides of economic cycles is not just a skill; it's an art form. Just as a skilled archer understands the perfect moment to release an arrow, stealth wealth practitioners possess the wisdom to capitalize on booms and busts, propelling themselves towards financial greatness. Life, like the market, is a symphony composed of various seasons, each with its unique melody. Understanding the periods of time and seasons is key to unlocking the secrets of financial success. Just as spring brings new life and opportunity, economic booms create fertile ground for growth and prosperity. Conversely, the chill of winter and the harsh winds of economic downturns present challenges and adversity. Yet, it is precisely in these periods of drought that hidden opportunities lie dormant, waiting to be awakened.

So, how do we spot emerging opportunities and fully tap into our wisdom to identify these periods of growth?

Well, it's simple. I've laid out three ways:

1. Embracing the Mindset of Abundance:

   To capitalize on booms and busts, you must cultivate an unwavering mindset of abundance. Recognize that the world is abundant, and wealth flows to those who believe in its infinite possibilities. Even during the darkest times of economic downturns, maintain unwavering faith in your ability to create and attract opportunities. Trust in the process, and abundance will find its way to you.

2. Courageously Learning and Innovating:

   During periods of drought, where resources may seem scarce, it's precisely the time to unleash your creativity and innovative spirit. Seek out untapped markets, identify unmet needs, and dare to pioneer new solutions. Great fortunes have been built upon bold ideas and the audacity to challenge conventional wisdom. Learning is the key to this, and the more you learn, the greater your capacity to innovate and create groundbreaking solutions. Embrace the thrill of uncertainty, for it is in these moments that legends are born.

3. The Power of Resilience:

In the face of economic storms, resilience becomes your most powerful weapon. Like a sturdy oak tree that weathers fierce winds, develop an unbreakable spirit that bends but does not break. Embrace setbacks as opportunities for growth, adapt to changing circumstances, and bounce back stronger than ever. Remember, the greatest triumphs often arise from the ashes of temporary defeat.

Intuition and Strategic Timing are also important when it comes to timing the shot. Knowing when to scale back and when to load up your metaphorical slingshot requires a delicate dance between intuition and strategic timing. Develop a keen sense of intuition, honed through experience and an understanding of market dynamics. Trust your gut instincts, but always temper them with careful analysis and research. The art of timing lies in seizing the right opportunities, striking with precision, and aligning your actions with the larger rhythm of the market.

1. Scaling Back for Momentum:

Just as a skilled archer pulls back the bowstring to gather momentum, there are times when scaling back is a strategic move. Assess the risks, review your financial endeavors, and streamline your focus. Shed unnecessary burdens, simplify your investments, and conserve your resources for the inevitable leap forward. Remember, the power of restraint can create a springboard for future success.

2. Loading Up the Slingshot:

When the stars align, and the market presents a clear path to success, it's time to load up your metaphorical slingshot. Channel your knowledge, experience, and accumulated resources into bold moves that have the potential to catapult you towards unparalleled financial heights.

3. Dry Seasons to Super Blooms:

The journey towards financial independence and accumulating wealth will undoubtedly face difficult times. These dry seasons can be discouraging and frustrating, but they are just as necessary as the super blooms that follow. The state of California experienced a prolonged drought that lasted for several years. This dry period caused a shortage of resources, impacting the economy and agriculture industry. However, after several years of drought and restrictions on water usage, California suddenly experienced a surplus of rain in 2019. This excess rain led to flooding, but it also brought forth a super bloom of wildflowers. Fields of poppies, lupines, and other flowers appeared across the state, transforming the landscape into a vibrant and beautiful sight to behold. This super bloom was a reminder that even in the toughest of times, there is always a chance for growth and renewal. Just as the dry season was necessary for the super bloom to occur, our financial challenges are often necessary for our growth and long-term success. We learn to appreciate the value of money, become more mindful of our spending habits, and focus on what truly matters.

> *"No matter how good you are in the game, the bad breaks come."*
>
> **- WINNING TIME**

During dry seasons, it is crucial to stay in peace and trust the process. We must remain calm and steadfast in our goals, even when it seems impossible to move forward. It is a time for us to be resourceful, find new ways to make money, and persevere with determination. Remember that nothing can snatch us out of God's hands. We are in control of our own destinies and have the power to create our own super bloom. We must stay positive, remain focused on our goals, and never give up. The dry seasons we face in our financial journeys are necessary for growth and renewal. Just as the super bloom only occurred after the prolonged drought, our financial successes are tied to the challenges we face. We must stay in peace during these times, trusting the process, and remaining determined to achieve our goals. With faith and hard work, we can overcome any obstacle and create our own super bloom.

Navigating Uncertainty with Purpose: Blending Hope and Faith

In the pursuit of living a life of stealth wealth, where equanimity and stoicism are prized virtues, the concept of hope and faith takes on unique significance. While I have emphasized the importance of action and facing challenges head-on, it would be remiss to discount the power of hope and faith in navigating the uncertainties that accompany our journey. Hope, often seen as a passive force, can indeed be misleading if devoid of action. It can create false expectations and delay the necessary steps towards progress. However, when paired with conscious action, hope becomes a driving force that propels us forward. It becomes the beacon that illuminates our path, guiding us towards the possibilities that lie ahead.

Faith, on the other hand, is hope in action. It is the embodiment of belief, trust, and resilience. When faced with circumstances that seem beyond our control, faith can offer solace and strength. It is the unwavering conviction that, despite the challenges we encounter, we have the capacity to overcome and adapt. In the realm of stealth wealth, blending hope and faith means adopting a mindset of active anticipation. It means acknowledging the uncertainties that exist but refusing to succumb to fear or paralysis. Instead, it involves embracing the notion that challenges are opportunities for growth and that we have the power to shape our own destiny.

To effectively blend hope and faith, we must first confront our fears and uncertainties head-on. It is essential to acknowledge the possibility of failure, job loss, financial setbacks, or the emergence of disruptive technologies. By facing these potential threats directly, we empower ourselves with knowledge and awareness. We open the door to understanding the risks involved and can then take strategic actions to mitigate them. Simultaneously, we nurture a sense of hope that fuels our determination and propels us forward. Hope allows us to envision a brighter future, even in the face of adversity. It encourages us to take calculated risks, make bold decisions, and persevere through setbacks. With hope as our compass, we remain focused on our goals while adapting to changing circumstances with resilience and flexibility. Faith acts as our anchor during times of uncertainty. It is the unwavering belief that we possess the inner strength and resourcefulness to weather any storm. With faith, we cultivate trust in our abilities and trust in the process of life itself. It enables us to maintain a positive outlook, even when the horizon seems obscured by challenges. Blending hope and faith within the context of stealth wealth means living with urgency and purpose. It means embracing the present moment while simultaneously preparing for the future. By aligning our actions with our beliefs and infusing them with a sense of hope, we create a powerful synergy that propels us forward on our path.

The path to stealth wealth is one that requires a delicate balance between action, hope, and faith. By facing challenges head-on, embracing hope as a driving force, and nurturing unwavering faith, we can navigate the uncertainties of life with purpose and resilience. This harmonious blend empowers us to live urgently, seize opportunities, and discover the true depths of our potential.

In the end, there is absolutely no better investment than in time, health, relationships, knowledge, and information.

STEALTH WEALTH: UNVEILING THE TRUE CURRENCY OF LIFE

As we come to the end of this extraordinary journey, it becomes abundantly clear that the truest and most profound investments we can make lie in the intangible treasures that shape our existence. In a world often driven by material wealth and the pursuit of external success, we must pause, reflect, and reframe our understanding of what truly matters.

TIME:

Time, the ethereal fabric that weaves through our lives, is a gift beyond measure. It is an intangible currency, flowing with ceaseless rhythm, ticking away the moments that make up our very existence. How we choose to spend our time determines the quality of our lives. It is in the quiet moments of self-reflection, the shared laughter with loved ones, and the pursuit of our passions that we find true fulfillment. Investing in time means cherishing each passing second, making each moment count, and savoring the beauty of the present.

HEALTH:

Health, that delicate and invaluable companion, is the cornerstone upon which everything else rests. Our bodies are temples, vessels for our dreams and aspirations. Nurturing our physical, mental, and emotional well-being allows us to navigate life's challenges with resilience and grace. It is in honoring our bodies and souls that we unlock the strength to pursue our dreams, make a difference, and embrace the fullness of life's experiences. Investing in health means treating ourselves with kindness, prioritizing self-care, and cultivating a balanced, vibrant existence.

REAL RELATIONSHIPS:

Relationships, the delicate tapestry of connections that intertwine our lives, are the very essence of our human experience. It is in the bonds we form, the love we give, and the love we receive that we find the greatest joys and triumphs. Our relationships have the power to shape our world, offering support, comfort, and the shared pursuit of growth. Investing in relationships means nurturing connections, fostering empathy, and embracing the transformative power of love. It is in the tapestry of relationships that we find belonging, purpose, and a profound sense of fulfillment.

KNOWLEDGE:

Knowledge, the timeless beacon that illuminates our path, is the key that unlocks the doors of possibility. In the pursuit of knowledge, we expand our horizons, challenge our assumptions, and embark on a lifelong journey of growth. It is through knowledge that we become empowered to effect change, to make a difference in the world around us. Investing in knowledge means embracing curiosity, seeking wisdom from every source, and recognizing that true wealth lies not only in possession but also in understanding. It is through the acquisition and application of knowledge that we become catalysts for progress and agents of transformation.

INFORMATION:

Information, the ever-present tide of knowledge and connectivity, is the tool that empowers us to navigate a rapidly changing world. In this digital age, access to information is abundant, but discernment and wisdom in its consumption are paramount. Investing in information means filtering out the noise, cultivating critical thinking, and using our newfound knowledge to make informed decisions. It is through the conscious consumption and application of information that we become catalysts for positive change, shaping a future that aligns with our deepest values and aspirations.

In the final analysis, the true essence of wealth lies not in the accumulation of material possessions but in the cultivation of a life rich with time, health, relationships, knowledge, and information. These are the intangible currencies that possess a value beyond measure. They are the invisible threads that weave together the tapestry of our lives, shaping our experiences and defining our legacy. By investing in these profound treasures, we not only enrich our own lives but also sow the seeds of a more compassionate, connected, and meaningful world.

May your journey through life be guided by the wisdom and peace that comes with building stealth wealth as you embrace the profound beauty of investing in time, health, relationships, knowledge, and information. And as you embark on this transformative path, may your heart be touched, your spirit ignited, and your legacy be one that echoes through the ages.

CONCLUSION

Congratulations! You've reached the end of "Stealth Wealth: The Ultimate Guide to Building and Protecting an Invisible Fortune." Throughout this extraordinary journey, you have gained an arsenal of knowledge, strategies, and insights that will empower you to achieve unparalleled financial success.

By embracing the power of information, you have discovered the hidden pathways to wealth that few others dare to explore. Armed with this newfound wisdom, you possess the tools to navigate the intricate web of the financial world, making informed decisions that will lead to long-term prosperity.

But knowledge alone is not enough. The true strength lies in discretion—the ability to wield this knowledge with precision and subtlety. You have learned the art of keeping your financial affairs hidden from prying eyes, shielded from the distractions and judgments of the outside world. This cloak of invisibility allows you to focus on what truly matters: growing your wealth steadily and stealthily.Remember, building an invisible fortune is a marathon, not a sprint. It requires patience, discipline, and a steadfast commitment to your financial goals. Armed with the insights from this book, you possess the blue-print to navigate the ever-changing economic landscape, adapting and seizing opportunities as they arise.

You now understand the importance of alternative investments, diversifying your portfolio beyond traditional options. You have learned the secrets of strategic debt management, utilizing leverage to accelerate your wealth-building journey. Tax optimization is no longer a mystery but a powerful tool at your disposal, ensuring you keep more of what you earn. The concept of asset protection has become ingrained in your mindset. You know how to safeguard your wealth, shielding it from unforeseen circumstances and potential threats. With a combination of legal structures, insurance, and prudent decision-making, your invisible fortune remains secure.

Yet, stealth wealth is about more than just accumulating material wealth. It is about achieving true financial freedom and living a life of abundance and purpose. You have discovered the mindset of those who have mastered this art—their ability to overcome challenges, embrace risk, and cultivate an unwavering belief in their own potential. As you close this book, know that the journey doesn't end here. The path to stealth wealth is an ongoing adventure, and you are the hero of your own story. Armed with knowledge, discretion, and a burning desire for success, you are ready to forge ahead and claim the financial future you deserve. Embrace the power of information. Embrace the strength of discretion. The road to wealth and prosperity is open before you, waiting to be traversed. It's time to step forward and embrace the limitless possibilities that await.

Remember, your wealth is invisible to the world, but its impact on your life and the lives of those you care about will be unmistakable. So go forth, dear reader, and let your invisible fortune flourish. The world is yours for the taking.

The true power of stealth wealth lies not in its concealment, but rather in its profound ability to silently and covertly transform lives. Allow your accomplishments to resound through the lives you touch, the organizations you support, and the communities you uplift. It is through these silent acts of generosity that your invisible legacy flourishes.

Jeremiah J. Brown is an accomplished author, investor, and consultant for high net worth individuals. He has a proven track record of success in identifying and executing profitable investment opportunities for his clients, and has built a reputation as a trusted manager in the world of finance.